_Transformation
of a
Walking Crow_

Transformation of a Walking Crow

by

Anthony J. Rodriguez, Walking Crow

©2024 Anthony J. Rodriguez
Cover Image and Design by Rick Schank of Purple Couch Creative
Photography by Donna Jean Shoemaker
Copyedit, Design, and Format by Diane Sova

All rights reserved.

No part of this publication may be reproduced, stored in a retrieval system, stored in a database and / or published in any form or by any means, electronic, mechanical, photocopying, recording or otherwise, without the prior written permission of the author.

ISBN 979-8-218-43591-2
Library of Congress #2024909950

Contact the author at
walkingcrow@sacreddrummedicine.com

Dedication

This book is dedicated to those who loved me and wanted to love me, doing the best they possibly could.

To my loving mother and original drum *Evangeline B. Rodriguez*, without whom I would have never been able to draw, breathe, and really, really know love.

To my father, in some places known as El Chaparito (the short one) and Un Pedacito de Cielo (little piece of heaven) *David G. Rodriguez*. He wanted to love me more than he could but didn't know how. If it wasn't for his example of not being able to stop drinking, I would have never been able to draw a sober breath and break the cycle of the alcoholism that has become "alcoholwasm."

To Rev. Emma Molina-Ynequez my Crow Mother, and to Diane Sova who holds the belief of an amazing friend. Thank you, thank you, thank you. I am truly humbled.

A'ho Shinawanahonata, A'ho Shiniwanahae!

Dedicated to those who suffer by their own hand and broken heart, that they may become open to their own healing and transformation. And to those who have no awareness of their suffering due to ego, may they find freedom from ego and self-obsession.

Thank you, Great Mother, Great Spirit, the love and guidance of the Medicine Wheel, the Four Directions and all my Relations.

A'ho Mitakuiasi!

Suffer no more, with love,
Your Son ~ Walking Crow

Foreword

"A journey of 1000 miles begins with a single step."
~ Lao Tzu

What started out as a weekly exercise walking around the Rose Bowl in Pasadena to the lush Descanso Gardens of the Verdugo Hills in California continued for more than two years.

Antonio shed pounds by the week, letting go of the past as he walked bravely into the unknown of what would lead to his life's work. As a shaman myself, I saw the signs. When we walked in nature, Antonio would stop in the middle of a conversation and kneel down to take a photo of a maple leaf floating along our path in a puddle of yesterday's rain. He would stop in the middle of a sentence to pick up a feather and then identify it as a hawk or a crow. I saw the path of the healer, warrior, sage, and shaman, to medicine man elder in every step.

One day I asked Antonio, "What is your spirit name?" He had not been given one. Our plan was to sit and ask the spirit world what his spirit name would be. Together we sat on a bench side-by-side under an ancient oak tree with our eyes closed. A few minutes passed and when we opened our eyes, much to our delight a jolly looking crow was walking towards him. We both laughed out loud as tears ran down our cheeks, simultaneously saying, "Walking Crow!"

On January 25, 2019, I was privileged to anoint Anthony J. Rodriguez as "Walking Crow," honoring the journey of a boy to Medicine Man.

Rev. Emma Molina-Ynequez
Lady Eagle-Feather

Preface

This short memoir was inspired by the magical and healing transformation I was willing to pay attention to and allow myself to say YES to. I became willing to accept my worthiness and the ability to stand and walk in my true power.

Writing this book never crossed my mind as I was always told how dumb and troublesome I was by the adults around me. Trying to understand my forever discomfort started to bubble up as I got and stayed sober over the years. As a child, I wasn't aware of the discomfort but the resultant anger, alcoholism, and drug use wasn't present in my life for no reason.

As I stepped into my new life and began to walk the Red Road (the path of my original native peoples), my eyes, heart, and soul began to open and soften to allow that long-forgotten little boy to breathe deeply as a spirit-filled man. Today I am *Walking Crow, Transformational Sacred Drum Medicine*, the embodiment of the little boy in the whole man.

~ Walking Crow
December 11, 2023
Sedona, Arizona

Transformation of a Walking Crow

Acknowledgements

I want to thank those that never believed in or thought much of me, as that strengthened my character. I am forever grateful to those who rolled the dice and took a chance by saying YES to me.

My nieces Kiana, Sara, and Halle	Grandmother Susan Stanton
My nephews Tristan and Jason	Jeanne Love
Angela Jeanne Hartnett	Kimberly Hodges
Armando	Luz Chacon
Astrid Barrero	Macehualli
Caesar G. Rodriguez	Marsh Engle
Carlos N. Iriarte	Master Sio
Chief Golden Light Eagle	Picos
Corey Jean Davidson	Rita M. Rodriguez
David B. Rodriguez	Sara Eaglewoman
David R. Hernandez	Stormy
Debbie Becker	Tata Luz
Diane Sova	Vanessa Leilani Adlawan
Dr. Gabor Mate	Wendy Jo Sperber
Dr. Theresa Smith	Xochitl Franco
Emma Molina-Ynequez	Yolanda N. Jimenez

The Mexico68 Afrobeat Orchestra
The Poverello Retreat Center
San Fernando Sweat Lodge
The Abyss
The Four Agreements
The Medicine Wheel and Knowledge of the Four Directions
The Star Nations
The Universe and all things it encompasses
Great Spirit and Great Mother
My Ancient Peoples
My Inner Knowing, Being, and Voice
Earth, Water, Fire and Air

Each of these people, places, and experiences profoundly affected my life and my BEING.

~ *Walking Crow*

Table of Contents

Dedication i
Foreword ii
Preface iii
Acknowledgements iv
Table of Contents v
Introduction 1
Chapter 1: Drastic Need for Attention 3
Chapter 2: A Desperate Child 9
Chapter 3: Struggle and Inner Conflict 13
Chapter 4: Behind the Wall 18
Chapter 5: Lip Service and the Power of Doubt 23
Chapter 6: Imposing Our Need 31
Chapter 7: Resolution/Restitution 37
Chapter 8: Nurturing Your Nature 71
Chapter 9: The Transcended Soul 76
Chapter 10: The Guide Within 88
Chapter 11: The Embodiment 94
Conclusion 98
About the Author 99

Transformation of a Walking Crow

Transformational Sacred Drum Medicine

Walking Crow

Introduction

Living and growing through young childhood into teenage years, there is much confusion and misunderstanding. We are unaware of the unseen scars we are left with through experiences with others, whether family, friends, teachers, clergy, political figures, strangers, religion, and even the media and television. "Oh, they won't remember." or "They didn't notice," adults would say. Even worse, traumatized youngsters might block such events out altogether, living in shame and hurt, deeply wounded. Some never come up for air from a myriad of addictions, psychological problems, or bad decisions that haunt them for a lifetime.

I was always told I remembered too much and to be quiet, labeled a bad seed and a problem child. How many have suffered from the poor decisions, behaviors, and extreme actions of well-meaning people that were supposed to love you? How could they, when they were wounded just as deeply, covering it up with numbing out or lies or the camouflage of the time? Have you ever wondered how that happened? How could that happen and nobody notice? Or did they notice and just not say anything? A lifetime of suffering and secrets… Shhhh! Don't tell anybody.

How many have suffered at the hands of colonialism and continue to do so? We all have, yet for the most part choose to ignore it. I feel like I have been fighting my whole life. In fact, I was - as an alcoholic for twenty years. I eventually stepped through the door of sobriety into a spiritual way of living that has changed my life and the lives of hundreds - if not thousands - of others.

I never felt a part of anything substantial in my life until I came to awakening. I found myself with my feet square on the Red Road, the spiritual path of my original native people. Even though I had never met them in real time, I found them deep inside of me as I said YES and moved through the spiritual abyss that has transformed my life, leaving me more powerful a man than I have ever been.

When will you get sick and tired of trying to do the right thing for people who tell you that you have to do something, without ever having done it themselves and admitting their failures? I am not a failure and never was. I don't believe in parroting the parrots, getting in line just to be another number or statistic.

I had to set myself free to find my own heart, soul, mind, and voice while standing on my own two feet. I found the strong shoulders of my ancestors and said YES to myself and to them. Are you ready? Do you want something new for yourself? Is there a better and different way of being?

I say YES to you and share my journey so that you can truly find yourself and begin to say YES after a lifetime of saying NO.

~ Walking Crow
Transformational Sacred Drum medicine

Chapter 1: Drastic Need for Attention

As a child, I felt different from the other kids. I was never tall enough, thin enough, light skinned enough, fast enough, or talented enough. I was picked last for everything. I was called names like nigger, spot, jasper, sambo, nigger lips – even by people who I thought loved me. Wearing 'husky' sized clothes and being labeled husky didn't help either, as it made me feel even more different, more isolated, and unloved than the other kids. I was a middle child, sandwiched between an older brother and younger sister. I didn't grasp pecking order at the time and couldn't understand why they were given things that I wasn't. My older brother was well groomed and dressed differently than me. My sister was dressed like a princess and honestly, looking back I felt slighted as a child. I didn't understand why I was so uncomfortable in my own brown skin and apparently carried that feeling around for many years, even into adulthood.

My father liked to refer to me as "prieto" which in Spanish means really dark-skinned. He might have called me that in an endearing way, but it never felt good or endearing and I hated it. It isolated me, making me feel more different and even unwanted for what and who I was. I don't know if my brother or sister ever felt this way, but I don't remember them being called names or being labeled like that. My brother and sister also make fun of my yellowish and crooked teeth. It really bothered me because it made me feel ugly. Was I? Was I really that bad and ugly? It surely felt like I was. Family always seemed to be the worst offenders.

My father went to the park every Sunday to watch the local soccer matches. He drank beer with his friends (or those who appeared to be his friends). I usually tagged along and tried to understand the game of soccer, but was exposed to a darker, more sinister game. It was my father's drinking. He got drunk nearly every Sunday, and it became habitual for him to be inebriated by the end of the day. I was terrified on the rides home as dad would stop to buy more beer or liquor to fill some sort of void that I had no idea about. He would buy me what I wanted, usually a 7Up and some Milk Duds, seemingly to pacify me. Then he would drive, swerving across lanes as I held on for dear life, terrified and wondering if we would make it home.

Finally arriving home, I could sigh with relief, feeling somewhat safer. My mom always had dinner ready for us when we got there. I could smell the delicious roast beef she was cooking in the oven, with mashed potatoes and gravy on the stove. The smell of food was always comforting after the long day and terrorizing ride home. Back in front of the TV, in my room, or out in the back yard, I was seemingly safe from harm. Or was I?

My dad used to tell me, "Your mom doesn't love you because you're darker than the other kids." Words like that were not a great thing to hear. I started believing him and noticed differences in how I thought my siblings and I were treated. It became more and more uncomfortable, so I never made any effort to be close to my mom and in fact drew away from her. I didn't realize it at the time, but dad was driving a wedge between me and my mom, brother, and sister. I don't believe it was conscious or on purpose, as he may have needed allies for his drinking (which my mom didn't like). Regardless, I was always willing to go along to the park, store, or anywhere that I could get dad to buy me some treat. It felt like a reward or prize for being his shadow.

Interesting that I used the word shadow to refer to myself. With all the names others called me regarding my skin color, I inadvertently began speaking of myself in this way. I didn't know it then, but I was craving attention. If that was how I got it, so be it…

I got in trouble a lot for saying things out of anger. Because of my lower status in the pecking order of the neighborhood kids, I was always picked last for baseball, football, or basketball teams, or not even picked at all if teams were already evened up. I usually sat on the sidelines, watching while they played. The neighborhood kids picked on me and made fun of me because of my size and lack of ability. It festered within. I had no idea why this happened to me; why would I? I was just a child! I felt like an outsider at school, in the neighborhood, and even in my family home.

One day, we were playing baseball in the street and an argument started between me and Richard Medoza. I don't remember what he said or even why we were arguing, but I called his mom a big fat pig. Richard got really upset and ran to my house to tell my dad what I said. This terrified me. I knew there was going to be a steep price to pay, and I would pay with my ass.

Sure enough, when I got home, dad met me in the yard, grabbed me by the arm and dragged me into the house, where I received one of the worst beatings I'd ever received. He took off his belt, put me tightly between his legs, and whaled on me for what seemed like forever as I screamed in agony. When he was done, I was sent to my room where I nursed the welts on my body. I can still see myself laying on my bed, touching my physical wounds and feeling utterly alone. Mom was at work, but I don't know if she could have saved me even if she was home.

This sense of feeling alone and abandoned later consumed me and was probably one of the reasons I picked up drugs and alcohol at such an early age. I didn't understand how my father could beat me so savagely. It wasn't the first and certainly wasn't the last time he did.

Writing this, I feel the sadness within for that scared, lonely little boy. Tears well up in my eyes, making it difficult to see the keyboard. I'm cold and I have a toothache. Not exactly surprising, with these memories coming up as I write. I didn't realize how desperately I needed attention. I sit here, deeply feeling sadness and grief about that part of my childhood. There were many complexities I could not understand. How could I? Nobody is given training or taught about these things when life lessons are being handed out.

There were many times I felt unwanted, rejected by friends and, most of all, by my parents. One time, when I was about three years old or so, I went with my father to the store. He was driving his '41 Mercury and as we came around the curve to our street, the door on my side (the passenger seat) flew open and I was ejected (rejected) out of the car and into the gutter. My father drove on, not even noticing I was gone.

When he glanced in the rearview mirror, to his surprise, he saw me running behind the car with our neighbor Clarence running behind me. Clarence witnessed my ejection (rejection) from the car as we turned the curve. Later, my parents took me to the emergency room to get me checked out and make sure I was okay.

It was a lifetime later that I realized I was not okay from that experience. These memories led to a path of healing from a childhood of not feeling loved with deep feelings of abandonment. Now, to be clear, I'm not saying I wasn't loved, I'm saying I didn't *feel* loved. Those kinds of things didn't happen to my brother and sister - or did they? I have no recollection of their potential traumas.

Another memory comes up, as a little boy with my mother at the kitchen sink. For some reason I was crying and clinging to her leg, wanting her attention. But she ignored me. I looked up and as she was washing the dishes, I saw she was crying. I remember thinking "Mom, I'm crying, too." I never knew what was going on with her that day, but she was again unable to give me her attention.

Over the years, it came to light that my mom's father, my grandfather, was a pedophile and a molester. This might have been why my mom was crying, as my grandfather often showed up at our house during the day for what I thought was lunch. I remember him sitting at the dining room table, drinking coffee and reading the paper. Or her tears may have been about my father's alcoholic behavior, I may never know.

My early life was filled with anger, sadness, hate, fear, and resentment. I had no idea at the time what this meant or to what extent those feelings festered in my body and mind. They formed the basis for my self-imposed suffering with self-hate, self-loathing, low self-esteem, no self-worth, and a host of other feelings stemming from not feeling loved.

As a child, I didn't know the language of love, or what love sounded or felt like. I don't remember ever hearing words of love or experiencing loving feelings from my family. I'm guessing, though, maybe at that time in the world love wasn't spoken of much, as war and unrest were the order of the day. I didn't hear about it or feel it, so how would I know what love was or what it meant? I mean, I heard about the love of God at the Catholic school I attended, but how could a guy stuck on a cross know how to love? His father sacrificed him to people who beat and killed him. What would my future look like? Hellfire and brimstone are what I was told I could look forward to. They call it hell, can somebody tell me or show me where the love is in that scenario? It seems I was destined for a life of mixed messages and that's exactly what I got. Everyone has a different excuse or story for causes of suffering and damnation.

People try to explain these things with dogmatic brouhaha, but I felt I was smarter than that, and that's why I was suffering. Jesus, it's said, taught in the synagogues and temples as a boy, and look how he ended up. I'm not comparing myself to Jesus, but I found myself to be a critical thinker at a very, very young age. I have always known things beyond my years but didn't know how or why.

It's like that in my life now. People who think they are better than me or know more than me sometimes question my critical thinking or put me down for not being educated their way or having some sort of advanced degree. There are many degrees of thinking and not just one school of thought, but some will try to convince you that *their* way is the only way.

As children, we were usually dropped off early in the morning at a relative's or grandma's house, then dropped off at school later in the morning. This was when mom was working day shifts. She worked in the aerospace industry and her hours would change from day shift to night (swing shift) to graveyard shift. When she worked swing or graveyard, dad took care of us, even though enjoying the flavor of the day - Olympia, Coors, Budweiser, Pabst, or whatever kind of beer he had, along with sips of whiskey.

He would, however, make sure we were fed, bathed, and put to bed. I remember him singing a makeshift lullaby to us called "uno mimi" which means "one sleep." As an adult, I wonder where he ever got the skills to take care of us, because he shouldn't have known how. It was a lifetime later, after I began my spiritual walk, that I was told by a psychic medium that my father was severely abused and even molested as a child. That answered some questions for me, explaining his drinking and violence.

Even with his behavior, I tagged along with him whenever I could, whether it was to the store, the mechanic's, a friend or family member's house, the church, or to the park. Dad seemed to find a happy drink wherever he went, be it Seagram's Seven, Canadian Club Whiskey, El Presidente Brandy, or beer. One day I went with him to the family mechanic's (who worked from his garage) and as we pulled into the yard, I was amazed about how huge his house was. The house itself wasn't so big, it's just that there was a fence around it, making it seem bigger. Getting out of the car, we walked over to the garage, where we found Emilio the mechanic sitting and drinking a beer. Apparently, he was sitting because he was too drunk to stand. He offered dad one, they had a short conversation (at least long enough to finish the beer), then we returned home.

With my dad, liquor never seemed more than a reach away. He would walk out the door and I knew where he was going. I'm not sure, thinking about it now, whether my brother or sister ever had any interest in those rides. Dad would buy his usual six pack, occasionally a bottle of whiskey and maybe some gum balls for me.

He usually watched Boxing from the Olympic Auditorium on television Thursday nights. Al Perez, a neighbor, often came over to watch with him while they had a few beers. I remember asking Dad to taste his beer. It tasted terrible, but almost every Thursday fight night I asked - always having the same reaction. Tasting that bitter, sour beer never stopped me from trying it again and again. By the time I was eleven, I was drinking beer and smoking pot, thinking that was what cool people did. What did I know about being cool? Nothing.

This eventually led to my own downward spiral with alcoholism, drugs, and food addiction. You see, the first bad taste or smell of something never stopped me from indulging – which contributed to those things becoming habitual. I would try anything. Well…within reason of my limited understanding.

Chapter 2: A Desperate Child

How funny…experiencing my lucid memory, I remember so much that most people would probably have forgotten. But what do I know about other people's memories? Every now and again when I mention something, my mother says, "Oh, sure, you remember that?" Do I have a selective memory? Was I forgetting other things? Or were the adults in my life resentful and angry because I do remember specific things they didn't want to remember and would never take responsibility for?

One night, as a three- or four-year-old, I was again awakened by yelling and arguing coming from the living room. I don't know if mom was working during this time, but that night she was home. I was scared hearing loud words and accusations I didn't understand, with my mother using extremely foul language. How did I know that was foul language at such a young age? Sitting here, knowing what I know now, I probably heard words like that even while in gestation in my mother's womb. A fetus hears and remembers everything it is exposed to from the external.

I stood, trembling and scared for my life and the life of my mother. My dad was trying to grab and hit her as I stood there watching. It's not clear why my brother David or sister Rita didn't wake up and I don't even know if they remember those arguments. Rita would have been too young to get out of the crib as she was only one or two years old. I don't think my parents even realized I was standing there as they were caught up in their whirlwind of emotional and physical violence, fueled by my father's drunkenness.

Violence seemed to be a part of my father's sense and lack of control. One night when I was about five years old, Mom was at work. He was angry because he couldn't find a tool he was looking for and assumed that one of us kids must have taken it. He lined David, Rita, and me up in the garage, then threw an orange and black nylon rope with a slipknot over the rafters. For some reason, I was first in line and he put the slipknot around my neck saying, "If you don't tell me where that tool is *right now*, I'm going to hang you from the ceiling." I don't remember what happened afterwards, but the memory of him with that rope around my neck stayed with me for a lifetime.

Years later, I developed a palsy in my right eye and had to wear a patch because it caused double vision. Wearing the patch allowed me to function in life and drive my car. My friend Lou Martin from Ireland invited me to do a live interview with him and remarked that my eye issue stemmed from repressed anger. It wasn't immediately apparent to me where this anger came from; I was unaware that the issue with my eye was due to a childhood trauma.

I sought out a healer friend of mine, Dana Maginnis, who had been helping me heal my body, mind, and soul from life traumas. Not long after the interview with Lou, I arrived at Dana's house for a healing session. I greeted her and Dana asked me to get on her healing table. I got on it and no sooner than I did, began crying uncontrollably. I was crying so much that my face, my collar, and the pillow under my head were soaking wet. Dana asked, "What's the matter, why are you crying?" I responded, "It's here!" "What's here?" she asked. It was the issue in my tissue, what it was that caused the palsy in my eye. The trauma that I had experienced as a child that evening in the garage with my father putting the black and orange rope around my neck surfaced as the palsy.

I had buried that experience deep in my memory. What had been pure sadness that my father placed a slipknot around my tiny neck and threatened to hang me had turned to anger and rage.

Dana asked if I was familiar with the Ho'oponopono, a Hawaiian prayer of forgiveness and healing. I responded that I was. She asked me to talk to my father and forgive him for doing what he had done that night in the garage. Repeating the prayer of forgiveness for my father, Dana then asked me to forgive the little boy who experienced the wound and to forgive the little boy for carrying the memory of that trauma for all these years. I began to do what Dana asked, repeating the Ho'oponopono over and over until I fell asleep.

Dana went to work on me and what seemed like hours later, I came too or woke up from an amazing healing. I no longer had need for the eye patch, the palsy cleared due to the release of the emotional trauma. I had been clearing traumas, hurts, wounds, and shame for others since becoming a healer myself, but this was the most profound personal healing I had ever experienced.

Violence seemed a part of my everyday life as a child, even in school. As a five-year-old, I was sent to a Catholic kindergarten school called Poverello of Assisi in San Fernando, California, the city of my birth. Now that I think of it, I was the only child from my immediate family who attended this school. I seemed to always be in trouble with the nuns there. They wore dark habits and a long rosary with Jesus hanging from it around their waist. It looked like some kind of threatening belt. There I was labeled a troublemaker, a bad seed. Those nuns slapped my face, pulled my hair, and twisted my arm while delivering what seemed like endless pinches to my skin as they jerked and shook me around vigorously.

One day, the nun who was teaching my class handed out papers, either home or class work. When I received my paper, it had a devil stamped on it, while other kids in the class had angels stamped on theirs. This stayed with me for a long time as I believed I was a devil. Confirmation of that belief came from my mother, years later telling me I had the devil in me. In hindsight they were labeling me as evil even then. I mean, who would do that to a child?

Years later, when I was writing poetry, I shared a poem called "Diablo Metido" (the devil in you) with my aunt Irma. She was shocked that my mother would say something like this, as she (Irma) had children of her own and was an educator.

My aunt Terri also reminded me that I was a troublemaker when I was little. When she repeated this to me as an adult, I stopped her and told her we were never to have this conversation again, that she was an irresponsible adult along with my parents and teachers, as I didn't raise me, they did. This! It left a seething anger in me for years.

Understanding my part gave me some relief but didn't comfort me during my 20-year bout with alcoholism and drug addiction. I don't remember ever being hugged or kissed or treated like a child - unless they wanted us to leave the room because we were making too much noise. There were mornings I remember mom taking us to school and stopping at the local donut shop to buy us one as part of our lunch. I loved days like this as I loved donuts – and her buying us one felt like love. Sometimes it would be lemon filled or raspberry or a long John twist or covered with chocolate. Wow! Such goodness. It felt like love, but in hindsight it was only filler and a pacifying gesture to keep us quiet. Or could I be seeing it wrong?

As kids, sometimes dad would take us to the Olympic Auditorium in downtown Los Angeles for Lucha Libre (in English, Free Style Wrestling). This was something we watched on television and every now and again dad would take us to this palace of what seemed like giants. Freddie Blassy, John Tullus, Black Gorman, and the Great Goliath were a few of the wrestling legends from my youth. Sometimes we didn't have to go that far as the local Devonshire Downs Fair Grounds would host wrestling events and we wouldn't even have to leave the San Fernando Valley where we lived in Pacoima. It goes without saying as we were being entertained and screaming with enthusiasm for our heroes, dad was self-embalming with the ever-present beer and whiskey. That was fine by us at the time because he bought us hotdogs, peanuts, and sodas. When the night was over, we would make our way home, not knowing if we would even make it as dad swerved back and forth across the lanes of traffic in his drunken state, our fingernails embedded deep into the truck or car upholstery from fear. It seemed there was always a price to pay for a good time.

Some of the good memories from childhood were darkened by my dad's drinking and ever-present violence. How strange to think that those things lived hand in hand and were part of what I had believed to be an amazing childhood. It wasn't amazing at all. Now that I look back, darkness and loneliness were the biggest parts of my life. Mom and dad were always working or having more kids. Dad's drinking and mom's enabling took precedence. I guess I can now say I was desperate to be loved and in hindsight a desperate child. I eventually grew into a man who still desperately wanted to be loved, but really didn't know what that meant or what love looked or felt like.

Chapter 3: Struggle and Inner Conflict

As an adult, I attended a family reunion at a favorite local beach in Ventura, California. While there, Hermie (sister to my aunt Terri) struck up a conversation and said she always felt sorry for me as a child. When she said this, I knew exactly what she was saying and why. She continued, "They always made you sit there (still) while the other kids played."

How wonderful it finally felt that someone saw what was going on, even though they didn't have the ability to do or say anything about it. I felt vindicated about my growing up, but that still didn't free me from my lifetime of suffering. It made me cry to know there was an injustice perpetrated on me and someone knew, vocalizing it after years and years. This might seem like nothing to some, but after years of blaming and silencing the child, I cried like the child I wasn't allowed to be. I cried for the little boy who felt like he was lost in the shuffle and never cared for or included.

Was I different? Was I wrong or was I broken? I didn't understand the why of it and as a child didn't have the capacity to know where I could get answers. A child doesn't ask these kinds of questions, why would they?

I didn't realize the world of shit I lived in until my later years. After my dad died on September 6, 1991, I was stopped by the police on my way home after another night of drinking. On December 6, 1991, I was taken to jail and charged with "Wet Reckless, DUI." It really was a DUI as I blew .08, far over the legal limit of .02. I didn't know it at the time, but that was the beginning of the end of that period in my life.

I went to court on January 3, 1992, where Judge Michael Knight of Division 101 Municipal Court in Van Nuys sentenced me to a $350.00 fine, 110 hours of community service, and twenty-six meetings of Alcoholics Anonymous. Somehow, because I was so hip, slick, and cool (so I thought), I was able to get out of two of the three parts of my sentence.

The twenty-six meetings of Alcoholics Anonymous was the scariest part of the sentence. This meant I would not be able to drink again - or so I thought. Self-doubt ruled my life. I thought I was slick and cool, but I really wasn't. I eventually went to a meeting, at a local church two blocks from my apartment. I wore my coolest torn jeans, a black overcoat, and a black beret. When I entered, there were only a few people there and I noticed all the chairs were little kid chairs, they were tiny. I guess that was appropriate considering how I was feeling about having to attend Alcoholics Anonymous meetings and the feeling of being small all my life.

The topic of that first meeting was about making amends, which I knew nothing about but spoke anyway when called upon. I said that I should make amends to myself for the way my life was. The person who was running the meeting felt he had to correct me and told me I needed to make amends to those I hurt. What? Did I just shit where I was about to eat for the next several years of my life?

Over a period of weeks, I got sober and eventually stayed sober, finding a home group and a sponsor to support my sobriety. My sobriety date was January 26, 1992. It just happened to be Superbowl Sunday. I went to a meeting that morning and later went to a Superbowl party at my cousin Joe's, the same cousin I had been drinking with the morning I was arrested. The morning AA meeting didn't help for the Superbowl party – or did it? I got drunk at the party that day, eating carne asada, drinking Tecate beer, and smoking pot. At half time the hat was passed for a store run to buy more beer. I tossed five bucks into the kitty and asked them to bring me a six pack of Diet Coke. Since that moment, I have not had a drink, pill fix, or any pot or cocaine.

I went to a meeting the next morning and raised my hand as a newcomer. I have never regretted my decision to break the chain in my lineage and end the cycle of alcoholism. I say that now, but then I had no clue that's what I was doing. I had never talked that way, nor would I know how to, but I know now. It began to free me from a lifetime of self-imposed suffering.

Not knowing what I signed up for, I heard similar stories and made friends with some of the most unlikely people. This distanced me even more from my family. I usually visited my mom for breakfast on Sunday mornings after my meeting and she would make me pancakes. I shared with her about getting arrested and becoming sober. When I mentioned my sobriety, her response was, "Don't be coming around here telling people they can't drink." Wow, I thought to myself, what a response. I remember telling mom that I was only sharing with her about my sobriety and the others were none of my business. There were things I felt I couldn't say and knew I could only speak to my AA comrades about not drinking. That was hard because I wanted my family to love, support, and care for me. I became increasingly conflicted and it marked the beginning of a long, hard struggle.

I understand my mother's reaction, though. She chose the drunk over herself and her family. That had to be a conflict deep inside. I don't believe the choice was really hers as I believe she was escaping something worse than being with my father. It eventually came to light that her father was a pedophile. I don't know what my mom's life was like as a young girl growing into womanhood, but it couldn't have been easy with a monster in the house. My grandmother had to know what was going on, but back then, because of Catholic beliefs you were stuck or trapped in a marriage bound by duty to the church and God. Choosing my father probably felt like the lesser evil for my mom.

I always wanted to be liked and wasn't sure what that would look or feel like in my newfound sobriety. My older brother sometimes approached me saying, "I saw so and so, they gave me their phone number to give to you." I would thank him and eventually throw the number away. I realized in my new way of living I didn't want to go backwards or have anything to do with my old life. Little did I know my old life went everywhere I did, as it lived within me.

I've run into folks from the old days and have even gone to see them in hospitals when they were sick, but that was the extent of my showing up or staying connected personally. For a couple of years, I lived out of state. When I moved back, an old friend from high school came to my mother's house where I was staying and invited me to a party. Against my better judgment, I went. It was nearby, in one of the neighborhoods I grew up in. When I got there, everybody was already drinking or drunk. They were people from high school, still speaking the same lingo stupidity they did back in the day. I found this to be more than I could tolerate, so I excused myself and never gathered with the likes of them again. I'm sure some are nice folks now, but I was out and far beyond the immaturity of childhood. Or once again, so I thought. I wasn't trying to be an asshole or anything, I was just done.

Isolation was something I eased into. I would get home from meetings or coffee after meetings and turn on all the lights, television or stereo, and get on the phone to talk to anybody that would talk to me. I found it difficult to be alone and quiet with myself, so always tried to keep myself busy. Stillness was not the order of the day…yet.

After getting sober, I got involved with what are called panels. I took AA or CA meetings to halfway houses, recovery homes, and other institutions. I took people with me, those who's sobriety I was familiar with. One time, I was doing a panel at a halfway house for men straight out of prison. I invited my friend Corey. After the meeting, she asked me how I could talk about my drinking like it was yesterday. I had been sober for some time by then and I responded, holding out my extended arm, "Corey, do you see the length of my arm?" She answered "Yes," and I told her, "That's how far away a drink is for me." I never forgot that moment and I have never, ever had a drink or used drugs again. My beautiful friend Corey has also stayed sober all these years and we remain good friends to this day.

One day, my friend JoLinda invited me to a church she had been attending. Actually, she had been inviting me for a long time, but I'd always had excuses or reasons not to show up. You know how we can be, evasive as all get out. I eventually showed up at the Church of the Valley in Van Nuys, California and was welcomed with open arms by the congregants. Jo sat next to me, proud and happy I was finally there. Come to think of it, I may have only shown up to church because I wanted to have sex with Jo. We had dated years before and remained close friends. I remember the sex being great, so why not? Both funny and sad now that I think back on it.

As I began attending church regularly, I had to unlearn the old regimentation of Catholicism. I shed the dirty old unwanted skin of the body of Christ, the genuflecting and crossing oneself, along with a myriad of prayers forced on us by colonialism, Catholicism, and the church. God, I had disdain for the body of lies they called religion. Speaking of hating it was speaking lightly, as the church and religion played a big role in most of my misery through my early life. Now, saying that and having the feelings I do about the church, why would I enslave myself with the same doctrine, just in a different dress? Good question!

Regardless of my past feelings, I spent years serving and being served in that church as a sexton, a caretaker, and a choir member. I believe I received more than I actually gave - and I gave deeply, from the bottom of my heart and soul.

Still there were trappings. I eventually left that church because I still did not trust completely. My inner conflict kept me rooted in this safe place, but I also wanted to run. Where would I go and who would want me? In the early days of my time at Church of the Valley, I often wondered why nobody came up to me, took me by the elbow, led me to the door and asked me never to return. Even as a grown man, I was having doubts about myself and why I was still here. I mean, didn't they know? Couldn't they tell? I had done things that Catholicism and God would never forgive me for (so I was told and believed).

The people at the church were very loving and forgiving. Old and young, woman and man, each nicer than the next. But I couldn't stay. My discomfort festered despite my sobriety, the church, God, and those fine people. I still carried deep wounds from childhood. Trapped behind a wall of struggle and inner conflict, I was still the child in a man's body with no clear way out.

This is a lot to admit and talk about out in the open, but it was and is necessary for the child to survive and eventually become the man, able to live in my thin skin.

Chapter 4: Behind the Wall

Being a man or pretending to be a man is not all it is cracked up to be. I still had issues and feelings of being 'less than' and 'not good enough.' Those feelings had not gone away nor was I able to grow out of them. According to society and television, men are supposed to be a certain way and have certain things by a certain age. I was married three times and never felt like I had anything to bring to the table. Why did I get married? Because society says that's what I was supposed to do. I eventually learned that there is no 'supposed to' or 'have to' in this world of mine.

Regarding the marriages, I didn't feel they were failed marriages, but I did feel like I was a failure as a man when it came to life. I had no positive example in my life to learn from. A drunken father was certainly not an example for following in his footsteps and nobody offered a hand up to a better or more fruitful life. Lots of people look to sports, television, politics, or movies for role models or heroes, but few are found as those facades are often exposed with subsequent falls from grace. Not the grace of a God or higher being, but the false and temporary grace of man. The person who can't find truth or power in him or herself will hang their hat on the hope of another, always looking for someone to save them or do it for them.

How many women hang their hopes on 'mister right' or 'mister right now' and are repeatedly disappointed by poor decisions, based on broken relationships with their father or emotional, physical, or sexual abuse when they were young? Men are no different and try time after time to live up to the tasks - or perceived tasks - at hand only to fail miserably again and again.

Men are just as or more broken than women but have a lot more pressure to succeed and provide. When did we start to believe the prevalent 'you have to…' and become failures to an invisible or false success? Who said?

I was lumped in this pile of broken souls trying to find my way out. Sober or not, I was trapped by the trap. Sobriety only insures sobriety. It also offers a never-ending trap of meetings and lost time for the real living in this world. We can become trapped by our own answers and solutions, not only our own but by someone else's, who has an interest in our soul's imprisonment. Church, government, Madison Avenue and the money machines of Wall Street and big pharma…this is what it is like to live or try to live behind the wall, a wall you can't see, but are imprisoned behind nonetheless. We somehow seem to live in this, steeped in alcohol, with drug addiction and addictions of every kind, broken relationships, abuse, and violence. Shit! Did I dream of this kind of utopia? I must have stepped out of line as they were handing out day passes to paradise.

Running around as a little kid playing football, baseball, and basketball I don't remember ever hearing the word alcohol or alcoholic. I do remember my parents talking about Emilio (our family mechanic) and how he stood in front of a liquor store because he wanted a drink so bad - but he wouldn't go in. I remember living that same struggle, wanting things that I couldn't or shouldn't have. Saying "I will never," but doing just what I said I wouldn't do. Cocaine was my darkest nightmare, but somehow, some way I walked away and survived it. I may have walked away from cocaine, but it was like changing my shirt and wearing alcoholism instead. Always fooling myself, I convinced myself I was fooling everybody else.

My own manipulation and the manipulation of others came easily, why wouldn't it? I learned from the masters put in front of me. Parents, grandparents, uncles, aunts, teachers, priests, nuns, politicians, police, neighbors, counselors, therapists, psychiatrists, and anybody else that wanted something from somebody. They all want something, don't they? The mouse wants the cheese, the cat wants the mouse, the dog wants the cat and so on. We all want something to make us happy or give us power, something we don't have to work for. Or at least I didn't want to work for whatever it was.

Trust did not come easy for me as the examples in my life had shown. Dad would never remain sober without drinking, mom would remain the enabler she had become, yet the adults around me found it easy to find, blame, and label the kid I was as a troublemaker. That was my biggest confusion. Weren't they teaching me something? Did they know how or what they were teaching me?

Because of my troubles in school, I was sent to a psychiatrist where he would ask questions and probe me for information. He had a Chutes and Ladders game, and we played while he asked me questions. One day he said to me, "Whatever you tell me is just between us." Boy was that a lie.

I didn't realize it, but when our sessions were done, as I exited his office through one door, my mom would enter through another. As I waited, I didn't know it, but the session would continue with my mother. I sat in the waiting room and pretended to read magazines. I was about eight years old at the time and knew how to read but didn't want to, so just thumbed through looking at pictures until my mother appeared.

One day, after a session we arrived home and my mother took out a belt and beat me with it. For me, this was a regular occurrence from her and dad - I never seemed to be a good little boy. Apparently, I told the psychiatrist that I had been searching in closets for Christmas presents and found them. He told my mother, after assuring me our conversations were only between him and I. From that point on, I lost trust in all adults.

Around this time, I was flunked in second grade. I always seemed to be in trouble there, too. Mrs. Gains was my second-grade teacher, and she was downright scary. She had a rough voice, wore thick glasses and a wig that her gray hair stuck out from underneath. She wore one-piece dresses usually worn by younger women, with her bra strap routinely hanging out. She always seemed to be angry, jabbing her finger at me and reprimanding or punishing me all the time. It was uncomfortable and downright scary.

Many times, I found myself playing my desk like a drum. This pissed Mrs. Gains off something else and was probably part of the reason I got flunked to repeat the second grade.

Being flunked meant something that I didn't know or understand until years later. My tribe had gone on without me and I was left behind to redo second grade with unfamiliar faces. Kids like Rickie Montes, Mike Arragon, and Pricilla Samaniego became Robert Lizaraga, Charlie Sanchez, and Joanne Culbertson. Such a confusing time for me, I didn't know what to do or how to deal with it. Not having close friends was a reality as I didn't get close to people, figuring they would go away at any time. This caused an unexpressed sadness that I didn't recover from until I stepped up and came into my power years later.

I could never really think about the future, I could only daydream about a life that was less than fulfilling to a sad and lonely little boy. I didn't really see my life as sad then. It was later, after a lot of living, marriages, and alcoholism, that hindsight revealed what was sad and painful. I looked at the other kids that went on without me and wondered what was wrong with me. Was I not tall, white, smart, talented enough, what was it? Confusion overwhelmed me. I wasn't the only one who was flunked, there was Vicente, Jaime, David, and myself. I never thought to talk to the others about why we were left behind or if they gave it any thought. Other kids, along with my siblings, called me a flunker or flunky and ridiculed me for my plight, making me feel worse about myself. Kids can be cruel. Kids always say shit to your face where adults talk, thinking you can't hear them. But I heard them. I always did.

I understand more and more as I write why my aunt Terri's sister Hermie felt bad for me and why her words were so comforting when I heard them as an adult for the first time. I mentally play the tape of that conversation from long ago and still find comfort in being seen and understood.

I still tagged along with my father, going to the park on Sundays to watch soccer while he drank. Even though I was terrified on the drive home at the end of the day, I still went because if I asked for money to go to the store, he would give it to me. As a kid some things were just worth the trouble, no matter the price one had to pay. Candy, gum, or soda's sweet goodness seemed my only comfort. I never saw the other kids from school at the park, in fact I never saw the kids from school outside for play days or anything like that. I was pretty much isolated with family. We were never invited to each other's houses; school was the only place we interacted.

There were times at the park my father came close to getting into fights. He and bigger men would get themselves behind trees so they could do battle. The bigger men, usually less drunk than dad, often had the sense to talk him out of the obvious beating he was about to take. Once, a man told my dad, "Your chamaco (kid) is here, you don't want to do this in front of him." My father was staggering and could barely stand, but I could see he was holding a beer bottle to hit the other man with. My father was a small man, only five-foot-one. I was afraid for the both of us, what would I do if something happened to him? I felt chills and my body trembled from the fear of his potential ass whoopin'. Sadly, I wasn't even a thought in my father's mind as he was too drunk to notice.

The day would end without a fight. The exercise of swerving across lanes of traffic would begin with my dad stopping at a liquor store, buying a bottle of whiskey or beer and a small 7Up and Milk Duds for me before making our way home.

It was ironic that dad's drunk driving took us right past the police station around the corner from our house. In fact, we had to go all the way around it to get to our street. Never thought about it as a kid, but as an adult, I worked to avoid the police when driving drunk - or thought I did - until the day I was arrested for drunk driving. As a matter of fact, one night I remember being so drunk I drove from Sylmar to Encino and, taking side streets to stay off the freeways, drove right by that very police station. I made it home safe that night, but my nervous system was a wreck because of the drive home. Funny, as they say, "A fool is not a fool until the fool shows himself."

Mom always had dinner ready when we got home and Sunday dinners were special. She would spend the day making roast beef, mashed potatoes, mixed vegetables, and sliced white bread with butter. Sunday nights safely at home was the best meal at the end of a long day for me. I never shared with mom or the others about the goings on at the park. I kept all that to myself until now.

Chapter 5: Lip Service and the Power of Doubt

I was slapped or beaten with a belt for saying what always seemed to be the wrong thing. I remember one time at my grandmother's house with my brother, sister, and some cousins. We were running around playing and got involved in a conversation about the FBI and how it meant Female Body Inspector. We giggled about that, unaware that my grandmother heard us. She called me in the house to interrogate me as to what FBI meant. I didn't know how to respond and got scared. I knew I was in trouble again and started crying, saying, "I don't know," while knowing that she had been listening or maybe one of my cousins told her about the topic of conversation.

Now, you must know my grandmother was a rosary and card-carrying zealot member of the Catholic church. She seemed to spend her time praying the rosary and taking care of us kids. My grandfather, being the predator pedophile, was probably the reason for all the praying. My grandmother was self-righteous and mean most of the time. Why wouldn't she be with a predator in the house? With all the information she held inside, she must have felt trapped, as the church has its rules and holds people hostage with them. Looking back, I feel sorry for her, at the same time asking, "Why didn't she say or do anything?" You can't live in a house as small as hers and not know what's going on. The old man was molesting my sisters, my cousins, and God only knows who else.

Oddly, my grandfather was respected and looked up to in the community. People either had to know what went on or they turned a blind eye. He's so smart, blah blah blah…I had no respect for him and stayed away from him. I remember things he said and did around cheerleaders at high school basketball games in front of me and my mother. I never said anything about that, because as a young teenager, why would I? My grandfather eventually died in his own shame and I frankly don't believe anybody misses him. Grandma died a few years later from a festering cancer, probably all that self-righteous judgment and anger had been eating her alive. That's what cancer does.

Cancer seemed to be riddled throughout my family on both sides. In my early twenties, my uncle Phil passed from tongue cancer, uncle Tony from lung cancer, and my uncle Charlie from ALS Lou Gehrig's Disease. My grandmother passed from cancer. My dad lived with lung and liver cancer and heart disease but died from heart failure. All that was probably due to his alcoholism and slow suffering over a lifetime. To this day I believe dad's heart disease and heart failure was due to his broken heart. This was my conclusion the closer I got to my life transition of becoming a healer.

I never had much to say about those deaths, my father being the most significant. Not much to talk about regarding the rest of them, other than for the most part my uncles were good people and probably gone too early. I did love them.

Whenever I was around family members, I didn't offer much information about whatever I was doing. As they say, "Know your audience," and that I did. Over the years, I drifted away from family members and gatherings, wishing and wanting something else but not knowing what. Being around family was a constant reminder of my pain and loneliness, which I didn't talk about. Drinking seemed the better option for comfort and that's exactly what I did - until that fateful day in December when I was arrested for the DUI.

Between getting sober and failed marriages, I was making bad decisions and had no idea how to choose differently. I was choosing jobs that should have raised my ego a bit, but my already low self-esteem suffered, continuing the vicious cycle of childhood without having the guidance or the education that I was told would give me something. But like a lot of barrio and ghetto kids, I had no idea how to get out or ask for help and was afraid somebody would find out how much I didn't know.

Fear ruled all my decisions, which is why I took up drinking and smoking pot. As an eleven-year-old I remember picking up a Pabst Blue Ribbon sixteen-ounce beer, drinking it and smoking pot in front of some of the younger neighborhood kids. I wanted to play big shot and be cool, but sadly I was anything but cool. I was in the middle of puberty and wore thick glasses, had a bushy haircut, dark brown skin and looked funny. I wanted to get together with the cute girls in the neighborhood, but what did that mean? I was taking my cues from television, watching all the cool people and what they were doing. I didn't know why I wanted to get together with the neighborhood girls, but in the old neighborhood where we originally lived, there weren't any. I mean there were girls in my old neighborhood, but they never came out of their houses and I only hung around with the guys.

When I was eleven, my family moved to a new neighborhood that was very different. No longer in the barrio, we moved to a middle-class neighborhood. They were friendly, white, some half white and half Japanese, some Mexican Americans like me. It was a whole different way of being and interacting with other people.

I remember hanging out with some of them and talking about kissing. What did I know about kissing? Shit! I was an expert (or so I claimed), pretending even at the age of eleven. I wanted to kiss Belinda Wisman, who was half Japanese and half white and knew nothing about kissing. Her sister Maria wanted her to learn and learn with me, which was pretty exciting for a kid like me (or any kid for that matter). We were going to practice French kissing or tongue kissing and when Belinda went to kiss me, she flicked her tongue in and out like a lizard, which made all of us laugh hysterically. I never really kissed her, but we grew to be lifelong friends.

I started working at a neighborhood liquor store at thirteen, making fifteen cents an hour plus all the soda I could drink. This meant everything to me because I would have my own money and wouldn't have to ask anybody for money. "No." was something I was used to hearing from my mom whenever I asked for money.

One time there was a track meet at a local high school and I wanted to participate, but how? At our school, we had a baseball field with an outfield fence and I taught myself to jump over it like a hurdle. Practicing by myself, I didn't tell anybody what I was doing, probably because I felt they would tell me I was silly. I was in the local Food King one day and saw a pair of sneakers for $2.99. These would be perfect for the track meet! I went home and asked my mom for $3.00 to buy the shoes. She said no. I begged and pleaded with her, saying that I needed these shoes and would never ask her for anything again. She finally said yes, gave me a five-dollar bill and off I went to purchase just what I needed for that track meet.

I knew nothing about running track or jumping hurdles, but I convinced myself I *had* to do this. It was inside of me and had a grip on me. I was going to do it. I excitedly went home with my cool new running shoes to show mom and when she asked for her change, I gladly gave it to her. That's where trouble began again. She looked at me with anger and asked where the rest of her change was. I gave her the exact change the clerk had given me. I didn't know what the problem was, but there was definitely a problem. The clerk charged me sales tax, which I knew nothing about, and my mother wanted exactly $2.00 in change as I had asked for $3.00. She ran me up and down about her correct change. What the heck? How was I supposed to know they would charge me more than the cost of the shoes? Deflated, I felt less and less excited about what I wanted to do.

Finally, she stopped bitching at me, but it didn't make me feel any better. My family has a way of holding things over your head to remind you at a moment's notice of some screw up. Come to think of it, there were never teaching moments of just talking to me. Nobody ever took the time to teach, but there was always time for yelling and ridicule.

Finally, the day of the track meet arrived. I put on my cutoff shorts, tank top, and brand-new shoes and headed to Bishop Alemany High School, a Catholic school I later attended. I made my way to the track field, waiting for my event to come up and my name to be called. I started feeling smaller or less than as I looked around at the other kids, who wore flashy track outfits and track shoes. I only had my cutoff shorts, a tank top, and my grocery store tennis shoes. Nobody at home knew what I was doing, but I ran into Michael Garcia from school. We said hello, he asked what I was doing there, and his only response was "Cool!" His reaction left me with my mouth hanging open.

This was it. The moment my name was called, and I made my way to the starting blocks. I was only running against one blond-haired kid who looked like he worked out with weights or something. The gun was fired and I ran like the wind, jumping hurdle after hurdle and finishing the race. He ran and hurdled like a gazelle, while I struggled to keep my legs and feet from hitting the hurdles as I jumped. The timekeepers took my information and made note of my time. I went home - there was no reason to hang around with nobody familiar present. I never spoke of that time with my family, nor did I feel I wanted to share my experience. Why would I? They didn't even know I was gone.

page 26

Working in the liquor store became my focus. My boss Jerry Rosenbloom, one of the owners, took me under his wing and began to train me, teaching me how to stock, stack, and put away beer and sodas, bag ice, sweep floors, and throw out the trash. I remember sipping my first free RC Colas, Mountain Dews, Cream Sodas, and others. I was a kid in heaven and could drink as much as I wanted. I also remember being paid for the first time and the feeling it left in my puffed-up chest. The other kids at school didn't have jobs but now I didn't have to ask anybody for money anymore. I worked in that liquor store for almost three years, until I was sixteen and old enough to work at McDonalds. This is where I fell into the trap of working as a young person, giving up my childhood and teenage years for money.

School was still problematic for me. I was mouthy and sarcastic and talked back. I couldn't mouth off at home for fear of a beating, but violence at the Catholic school was always present or looming as well. The trouble I would get into more than anything stemmed from the fact I was funny and would say what most wouldn't. Don't know if I was fearless, stupid, or both.

One principle, Sister Margerie, was an Irish nun from Massachusetts. I used to love to get her to say Massachusetts because as a Mexican American kid from Pacoima I got a kick out of hearing her talk. But I didn't like the attention I drew to myself because she would sink her principal teeth in and not let go. She didn't dress like a nun or wear the traditional nun warrior gear with the rosary belt. She wore skirts, a light sweater and short boy's haircut. When trouble appeared, that woman could point at you and snap her fingers with one hand at the same time. That kind of thing intrigued me. Where did she learn that, was it some kind of a teacher ninja thing?

I was never a bright student, which is definitely why I acted out. There were much smarter people in class, always the same ones: Joe Tortie, Joanne Culbertson, Brian Haynes, and others. It was just too much work to keep up and much easier to goof off than to buckle down and do something. I just didn't want to! Math was the problem of the day. If there was anything I hated, it was math. Like speaking to me in a foreign language with a southern drawl, it made my head spin. Homework was a nightmare. Multiplication was my nemesis and when that was eventually brought to Sister Margerie's attention, it was no fun.

What happened next made me hate her. When it was close to the end of the day, she pulled me out of class and made me follow her around as classes let out. She made me recite multiplication tables as we walked the halls. I was embarrassed and the other students laughed at me when they realized what was going on. It made my life miserable and if I could have, I would've kicked her ass. It all added to my fears and life embarrassment. I did not want people to know I was dumb and the adults around me made every effort to let them know I was. I was trapped! I never noticed whether this happened to anybody else around me or in my classes. I have no idea how I mustered the energy day in and day out to meet the humiliation of the day.

I often wondered where the love of a compassionate God or Jesus was in all of this. I mean, hypocrisy seemed to rule the order of the day, always. Never a teaching, a talking to, a lesson or anything other than ridiculing me and making me feel like a stupid failure.

I was kicked out of that school at the end of sixth grade and sent to George K Porter Middle School in Granada Hills, a public school in an all-white neighborhood where I had never been. Public school was something I had only experienced once at a summer school at Haddon Avenue Elementary School, in the Mexican American neighborhood in Pacoima. Seems my comfort zone was with the Mexican Americans as this was all I had ever known except for the few Irish, Polish, Italian, and Japanese sprinkled around my old neighborhood. To me, we were all Mexican American. I didn't know any better and didn't care.

That summer, they taught us Mexican and Aztec culture, about the pyramids, Quetzalcoatl, Teotihuacán, and the wondrous Aztec civilization. This was awesome, something interesting about my heritage that I could relate to and feel proud of. It made me puff up my chest a little as I could see and feel myself in these peoples of the past. Such things were never talked about at home. I don't know if my parents or brothers and sisters knew about what I was learning. It allowed me to look at myself differently. I didn't feel myself as a dirty wetback, beaner, or whatever indignant and insulting name people like me were called. I was a proud indigenous person of a land I had never known, and I carried its spirit in my soul and in my bones. I will never forget those days in class. I still remember the faces of the other students and where I sat. How powerful a memory, how powerful the boy.

I only found myself in trouble once that year at Porter Junior High. We were in P.E. (Physical Education), playing kickball. Class was ending and our teacher Mr. Cameron asked us to pick up the gear and bases off the field and take them to the P.E. office. We started throwing stuff around and I threw a base I had picked up like a frisbee. It flew up on the roof and Mr. Cameron saw me do it. He pulled me into the office and called my mom because he was going to punish me and give me a swat with a huge paddle the coaches kept for hard cases like me.

He called my mom and told her what I had done. Her response was, "Well, if you think he deserves it." What did she say? That wasn't permission! I felt hopeless and fearful for my life. I was asked which coach I wanted to swat me, to add insult to potential injury. I chose Mr. Cameron because he was the smallest of the coaches. Big mistake. Mr. Cameron was buff and this grasshopper chose poorly. He took me into an equipment room, had me lean over a table, pulled his arm back and let loose. Holy fuck did that hurt! To this day I don't remember what happened afterwards, nor do I want to.

True to form, my mother didn't take responsibility, leaving my fate in the hands of somebody else. "If you feel he deserves it!" Shit! What about how I felt, didn't I matter? Apparently not. As I sit here writing, I notice that the base word of "apparently" is "parent." How ironic. My parents had relinquished their parenting to others who didn't know anything about me. Actually, my parents didn't know much about me either. They didn't ask how I was, or if I was okay. They lived in the bubble of their drunk and enabling world.

I was eventually let back into the Mary Immaculate School to go through the eighth grade, my final year of torture in that institution. Mrs. Edeman was my teacher for that year. You must know, this place was the source of most of my troubles, never mind that the drunk and the enabler at home were not great parents. They felt it was the school's job to teach us something and pretty much washed their hands of the responsibility to raise their own kids, blaming us when things didn't go right.

That final year back was reserved for the last bit of self-imposed humiliation I would suffer by my own hands or mouth at the hands of a teacher. Something I need to explain, back then I didn't know how to be quiet or to close my mouth when it was time. I was always trying to be funny, to defend myself and talk my way out of trouble. I was my own worst enemy and only got myself in deeper with my big mouth, trying over and over again to explain myself out of situations. You think at some point I would have learned better.

My friends and I were mugging one day in class as we sat in the back; that's exactly why we sat in the back. I must have gotten a little loud because I was singled out and called to the front of the class where Mrs. Edeman started reprimanding me. Once more, I tried to explain and defend myself which never, ever - and I mean never - helped my cause. I didn't stop when she asked me to be quiet and she finally slapped me right in front of the whole class. It wasn't a slap per say, more like a tap on the cheek, but just enough to embarrass me in front of everybody.

I ran out of the class, not knowing where I would run to. She followed me and demanded I stop. Against my better judgment, I did. I was no longer in front of the class, so felt better about my talking, as they weren't looking on. She was pissed and in hindsight had every right to be. I was disrespectful to her in front of the class, she took the only recourse she could so I don't and can't blame her. She apologized for slapping me and asked me to behave myself and be quiet in class. I heard myself say "Okay," and we walked back into class, embarrassed and all. I sucked it up and nobody in class ever mentioned anything about that incident. Ever.

Chapter 6: Imposing Our Need

When I got sober, I started remembering things. Being in the car while my father was drunk was a strong memory because it scared and scarred me for a lifetime. One would ask, how would that scar you and why? This is something you have to live through to understand. I was petrified every time I got into that truck on late Sunday afternoons. But my need to feel special by getting goodies from various liquor stores, I thought was worth it. Looking back, I couldn't say no to myself. I also felt a need to be there to take care of my dad. Where did I ever get the idea that I could or should take care of my dad? How would I or could I do that? My father had no ability to protect himself, much less me. The confusion and turmoil ran deep, and I can see the lonely little boy sitting on the bench seat of the truck alone and scared.

When I was eleven, my family took a vacation trip in the car up the California coast to Spokane, Washington to attend the World's Fair. I remember my father always driving with a can of beer between his legs. I don't remember mom ever saying anything about it, but she may have been preoccupied taking care of my youngest sister Yolanda. She was not even a year old, and mom had to keep us quiet to not anger my father. One night, making our way down the coast heading home, my dad was pulled over with all of us in the car. The officer didn't give a reason for pulling him over, but he talked to my father about how he was driving a steady straight speed limit. He probably suspected my father of DUI but didn't make him get out of the car after seeing all us kids in there.

My feeling, all these years later, is that my father dodged a bullet because of us. These memories are so clear, I remember them like they were yesterday. I still have a sense of the California Highway Patrol officer who stopped us and, although it was over fifty years ago, even remember his hand gestures. I can also visualize the scene from the perspective of the officer's car and can see the officer standing at the window on my father's side of the car and the tops of our heads as we sat in the back seat.

My realization that I felt somehow responsible for my father came over me with great anger and frustration one day as I sat in an AA meeting. I had shared this at a meeting because I heard one of the regular women talk about how kids never remember what's going on when adults are drunk. The fuck they don't. I raised my hand to speak for those of us who suffered at the hands of dangerous and suffering alcoholics. I know because I was one of them. I wanted to tell her to fuck off, there are always those who assume to talk for others but don't know what the fuck they're talking about. I don't speak for others, I am an advocate for others and support them, but never speak for them. My voice is mine and I speak for me and no one else. In my world, you had to put in your own work. Nobody did shit for me, no one ever spoke for me, why would they? If this feels angry to the reader, it is because it was buried for so long. I kept it deep and carried that anger until I couldn't or wouldn't anymore.

Why did I have to ask? Why did I have to need? Why did I have to want? Why wasn't I treated like the other kids at home? So many whys and tears. They never asked, or so it seemed. Was it because I would tag along with my father and was somehow being punished? My father's voice and the things he said to me about not being loved by my mother rang in my head, loud as ever.

In hindsight I know that wasn't the case, but when you're a lonely, husky, dark skinned kid and you are not so cute, one questions the self. Yeah! That shit was in there and it was deep. I remember having angry fits because I wasn't invited or included in games. I would throw things or do some kind of damage. The only person I remember hurting was myself, as it always ended up in an ass whooping. Ass whoopings were big in my family. Each parent had their weapon of choice and I'm not kidding when I say weapon. When my mother was angry and it was whoop ass time, she pulled out a wire fly swatter that was always nearby. That shit stung and left welts on our arms and legs. My father, on the other hand, used a thin leather belt. It was the sixties and that was what men wore. He would put me between his knees and squeeze tight. Looking up, he seemed ten feet tall with his arm in the air and the belt waving in the wind ready to strike. When it did, oh shit! Look out buddy - there was not one strike or even five or ten, it was all out war. Something probably snapped in his mind once he started, because there was no stopping him and there was no "This is gonna hurt me more than it's gonna hurt you" kind of thing. Nope! He would beat me senseless.

I can say this about my parents: he was an alcoholic running from whatever pain he was running from. She was the enabler running from whatever pain she was running from and "BAM" they ran into each other, got married, and irresponsibly had children. Why two people coming from their perspective situations wanted to have children, who knows. But they did and here I am, writing about our painful lives. Not sure if my siblings felt or experienced the same thing I did, I don't ask and frankly don't care. I was taught not to care or ask by trickle down. They say shit rolls downhill and this is a case of it rolling. It's not that I don't care about my siblings. My question is, did they care?

My dad was born December 29, 1918, in Rock Island, Illinois, son of Ramon Joseph Rodriguez, who worked in the U.S. for the railroad in the early century, during the time of the Mexican Revolution in Mexico. I don't know if I ever saw or knew my grandfather. My grandmother's name was Petra Gonzalez and I know very little about her, although I remember her being very indigenous looking.

The only thing I know about my father's life is that he was severely abused and lived with his mother in poverty, which might explain his alcoholism. My mother was born June 14, 1937, at General Hospital, Los Angeles, California, daughter of a pedophile who will remain nameless. He was from the border town of El Paso, Texas. My grandmother Carmen Macias was born in Metcalf, Arizona. She was a talented, interesting woman who was strong and angry and a devout Catholic. I believe her to be a Zealot, the way she prayed. Why wouldn't she be, married a pedophile with no way out except for prayer. I recently looked up Metcalf, Arizona and it no longer exists, less than a ghost town. I'm surprised I even found a trace.

Praying always made me uncomfortable because of how I was forced to pray. I never prayed to a god or anything. I only prayed - or pretended to - so they would leave me alone. My grandmother would make us kneel for what seemed like hours to pray the rosary. That shit felt like punishment. She didn't do it from a loving or a devout place, it felt desperate and empty, just performing a duty. I always say, "Duty is no reason to do anything." If I didn't pray the right way or sat back on my heels from the kneeling position, I got pinched and scowled at. It was pretty scary. I don't know if she meant to be, but my grandmother was scary, too. She wore a scarf on her head and held her rosary fiercely as if her life depended on it. She was a warrior for desperate prayer, holy cow! But I can see how her life depended on it with my grandfather in the house.

School was no different. From the youngest age, I remember being forced to kneel and pray to Mary, God, and Jesus. Why? What purpose did this serve? The nuns were just as violent and angry as my grandmother, they must have met in secret huddles or religious circles to plan their actions of force upon the world. The level of hair pulling, arm jerking, pinching, slapping, and suffering devout torment both at school and at my grandmother's house was more than one should bear as a five-year-old child. Their methods of indoctrination would live in my skin, bones, and heart for years. What had I done in my early life to deserve this kind of treatment by people in the name of their God?

We were often marched into church to experience forced spoon feeding of genuflecting, kneeling, standing, praying, and sitting through repeated lectures - only to repeat over and over and over again! The church and its people were so full of themselves. Those who were compliant would walk into church with their hands dutifully folded, palms together in the golden light position in front of their sternum, like a painting of a saint or something. I was always aware I was being watched and never felt God wanted us to do this out of duty. Even as a child I believed that God didn't want me to be motivated by thinking these actions were our duty.

When my mother went to church on Saturday afternoons, she would say, "I'm going to do my duty." Really? I remember thinking what does that mean? How stupid do you think God is? She would write a check for five dollars to put in the basket and head out the door. Catholics and others say that kind of thing because they don't know how to unbelieve or unlearn what they've been taught or what's been forced on them. I believe this to be part of the five hundred years of colonialism in what's known to me as the Americas. Somehow Europeans got it up their ass that peoples and cultures thousands of years older than theirs wanted or needed to be spoon fed God, Jesus, and Mary with a shovel, only to murder, steal, and claim the Americas as their own by destroying and decimating ancient cultures. I have a hot button about this inside of me. It's who I am despite being seventeen percent Spanish.

Expressing or referring to God as "HE" was always another tick under my thin skin. Thin because everything bothered me, hurt me, or was questioned by my heart and soul. I have always been sensitive and felt way too deeply. I felt your anger through hate, sadness, violence, loneliness, the belt, rope, hanger, fly swatter, hand, paddle, and other punishments. Why wouldn't I feel that when it was taken out on me? Why did I have to be the lonely part of the mess created by you saying yes to such a wounded man, wounded woman? I felt like a pawn between my mother and father. My mother had nothing to do with that feeling, but father saying to me, coming from his own childhood (or lack of one), "Your mother doesn't love you because you're darker than the other kids." That hurt me deeply.

It was here that I knew his statement was bullshit. My dad was way darker than me and my mom loved him, as much as he pissed her off. Why wouldn't she love me? Why would he insist that I wasn't loved? His self-esteem must have tanked and the only bravado he could muster was through the bottle. But he said this more often than not and those words never left my core, even though I knew mom loved me. Didn't she?

Because I was small, I was picked on by bigger kids on the school playground. When that happened, I would go running for my older brother or ask somebody to go get him. He would come running and scare the shit out of that bigger kid. My brother Dave was way taller than me and lanky thin. I can't tell you how many times this happened as a kid and even as a young adult.

One time we were having a party where we lived and this guy showed up named Wes. Wes was the boyfriend of my friend Terri. Somehow Wes got it into his head that something was going on between Terri and me. What, we can't simply be friends? Apparently not! Wes was drunk when he came in and made a beeline for me. I didn't let him talk, him being the taller of the two of us. I reached up, grabbed him by the collar, and started pounding on his face. It left him defenseless. My friends and brother saw what was happening and like a swarm of wasps, they were all over Wes, who had no idea what was happening. They picked him up and threw him on the street. I never saw him again. My friend Terri couldn't stop apologizing, she was so embarrassed.

I imagine my father, being small in stature, probably went through the same type of thing as a boy or young man. He would often take us into the yard and try to teach us fighting moves. In hindsight, the moves he tried to teach us would never work in a real-life scenario, they were more like television wrestling moves which only work with practice and in the square ring. Real life was way more complicated than that. Violence was never far away and maybe I chased it, who knows? I was at the farthest point of our school yard once, when I saw another kid from my class named Manuel. In my hand was one of those big combs, which I thought was cool. Oval shaped, it had a ring to slide over my finger and had very short brush-like bristles, for men or boys like me with very short hair.

I don't remember what I said to Manuel or what he said to me, but I took my hand with the comb in it and hit him across the face, scratching him. He started crying. I began to panic and apologize profusely. When he finally stopped crying, I kept apologizing and asked him not to tell anyone. Manuel was a sweet kid and didn't deserve that, no one did. Manuel never told anybody that I know of about it to this day. I had become a bully, when all I wanted was to be liked, loved, and cared for. Where would I find the words for that and who would I ask first? What a lonely existence I was having at only eight years old.

I remember seeing Manuel at a distance years later and he looked like the same sweet kid I assaulted years earlier. I still felt terrible and riddled with shame. I never approached him out of shame and embarrassment. How could I? Inside I was still that wounded little boy not being able to escape himself.

Chapter 7: Resolution/Restitution

Not knowing my place always seemed to be a problem for me. It was like I was living my life outside a fishbowl and every now and again jumping in, only to find I couldn't swim. For most of my life, I dog paddled in the shallow end until I eventually stepped into my medicine and began to broad stroke and swim in the deep end without fear.

Work and school were like that for me. I loved working, was never late and learned the job to the best of my ability. My first job at thirteen in the liquor store was where I learned warehousing, a skill that served me all my life. I was always a good employee. At seventeen, I went to work at Chief Auto Parts and before long I was making more than three times the minimum wage. I was making seven dollars an hour in 1978 and the minimum was about $1.98. I had health and life insurance with quarterly and cost of living raises. Why I didn't stay there, I'll never know. From there I went to work on the docks of Industrial Freight Systems, loading and unloading trucks for the same money. I was one of the youngest guys on the night crew and worked a part time shift from five to ten pm with my friend Richard.

While I worked, I still attended school which was never important to me. In high school I had my own money and didn't have to ask anybody for anything. I was sharp and well dressed. I wore nice clothes from the mall stores and great shoes, while other kids in school wore what their parents could afford. I drove my parent's car everywhere I went and claimed it as my own. I did all the repairs, even replacing the engine without asking them for the money to pay for it. I special ordered the engine because I worked at Chief Auto and great discounts were a perk. I believed all this was cool and that I was cool, so being cool and having money became the most important thing to me.

Money does strange things to people with their egos and I was a case of that. My mother saying "no" to me while buying things for my brother and sisters had a huge impact on me and changed my life forever. I remember her coming to me and saying, "If you quit your job, I'll give you five dollars a week." I was making $140.00 to $200.00 a week at the age of seventeen. Why would I say yes to that? It added insult to injury. I was highly aware of the family pecking order and I wasn't part of it. I was too cool for that and didn't want to be controlled by their money.

Transformation of a Walking Crow

In my first years of high school, I went to the Catholic Alemany High School and played saxophone in the marching band and orchestra. I had to take an entrance exam to get into the school and one day realized they put a whole group of us with Spanish surnames in remedial classes. Remedial! Really? I was no shining star but had been reading and doing math since I was six or seven years old.

One day I was sitting with an older student who I was sent to for tutoring in reading. I remember him talking to me like I was an idiot and me thinking, "This guy is stupid, why is he talking to me like that?" At some point, he realized that I knew how to read and was somewhat embarrassed by the way he had been talking to me. He said, "You know how to read, why are you here?" That's when I realized what the racist Catholic school had done. Just because we had Spanish surnames didn't mean we were stupid. Wow! Without apology, the school leaders then moved us to classes with the rest of the school population. There wasn't one white kid in any of those remedial classes.

I loved the marching band, and played at football and basketball games, even traveling to do community parades. I loved it and actually felt a part of something. One aspect I didn't like was playing school concerts where we were supposed to dress up and wear a suit and tie. Even though I was making my own money, I certainly didn't want to spend it on a suit for school. Let my parents pay for that, they sent me there.

Once we had a winter concert and I showed up in jeans and a linen shirt with color designs around the collar and chest. We were supposed to wear suits and be well dressed. The band director gave me a dirty look, but I pretended not to see him. Out of the corner of my eye in the dark space of the hall, I saw my parents enter. They sat against the wall near the door. As usual, dad was staggering drunk and I was embarrassed. So was my mom, she had to be! This seemed to be the old man's role. I was surprised they were even there, as usually they didn't show up for me when I played music. I also remember my father saying to me that I didn't really play music, I was just out fooling around somewhere. How would that drunk know anything about anything?

After my second year at Alemany, my parents decided to remove me from that school and enroll me in the local San Fernando High School.

Transformation of a Walking Crow

When I asked why, I was told that they could no longer afford to send me to Alemany. However, they could afford to leave my sister there (she was later expelled for being drunk in school). Yeah, right! Who said life would get easier or be fair?

Again, I was separated from my tribe. This happened a few times during my school years and it didn't feel any better this time around. As a seventeen-year-old, I didn't know enough to understand what being separated from my tribe meant; I didn't even know I had a tribe. It was years later, after all the drugs, drinking, gorging, and womanizing stopped that I understood what those years did to my soul, body, and mind. I went to San Fernando High and enrolled in classes. When I did, I was so desperate not to be a nineteen-year-old senior that I registered as a senior, hoping I could somehow skirt the system, skip a year, and nobody would notice.

I was sharp in every aspect of my life, but not sharp enough for the system. It was as if I lived in two worlds yet couldn't even live in my own skin. Saying I didn't have a clue about tribe separation at the time, I realized I was lying to myself. Darkness and desperation forced me further into working, making money, and just wanting out.

While working at McDonalds as a sixteen-year-old, I got involved with some fun characters. They were barrio kids like me - cholos, partiers, pot heads, brainiacs. We had such a great time at work, it wasn't like working at all. Between the guys at work and school, time off was fun. We all wanted to act older and we liked to drink beer. We would play these crazy pick-up football games at a place called Chase Park in Panorama City. We were a rough and tumble band of boys and played killer tackle football games. We took no mercy on each other and for the first time in my life I really had a place with young men who called me friend, buddy, esse, home boy, Anthony, Tony.

As hard as those games were physically, I couldn't wait to play. I found there was no being picked last or not at all, we all had worth and everybody played in that sacred circle of young men. At that time, I knew nothing about sacred circles, so for me to look back and make that reference is really a big deal. We were mighty, brave, tough, smart, funny, brown, black, Asian, white, we were equals on the grass field and the only price for our toughness was a cold beer at the end of play.

Having this group of guys was still not enough, as I often found myself between events at school, work, or play feeling the loneliness of my life. As I moved between groups, one of the groups I fell into was musicians and over time we formed a band named "Spirit." In hindsight, I have to laugh, because spirit was trying to get my attention even then. Being in the band with these fellas gave me status, it was like the group of guys I played football with. In fact, some of them were those guys, there seemed to be overlap. We played top forty and jazz at parties and dances.

But more than anything, we played for ourselves because of the kind of music we played. We were fusion players, but the student body and general public didn't seem to care for our style of music. Fusion was a style of jazz we loved, and we were able to showcase each other through solos and some bad ass playing. The band eventually broke up and we went our separate ways. I can't tell you if I had any feelings about the band breaking up, I was really just glad to be able to have had the opportunity and ability to play with them.

The time came for senior pictures and I asked mom for money to buy a suit. She offered sixty dollars and told me to buy a blazer or jacket. That hurt because I remember her buying my brother a number of suits, but never one for me. It didn't seem fair, but again what does fair have to do with anything? I eventually purchased an outfit of some kind and had my pictures taken, which was strictly an exercise in futility because deep inside I was looking for a way and reason to leave. I knew I would never graduate high school if I wasn't with my original tribe. I did not want to be a nineteen-year-old senior and when that time came, I was making my exit. It never occurred to me that I could just walk out and leave and never come back. I felt there would be a steep price to pay for just walking out. I hated being there and with every day that went by, I got more uncomfortable.

How could I explain it to mom and dad? What would my friends think? And what would I do for work or even for the rest of my life? I had already said "no" to dad when he asked me to go to the union and apply for a job with General Motors in Van Nuys, California where they built Camaros. I didn't want to offend dad, so I thanked him for all his job at the plant had given us and the home it created, but no thank you to working there.

There were a lot of reasons I didn't want to work there. The main reason was the place was filled with alcoholics and drug addicts and I didn't want to be one of them - even though I was already drinking and smoking pot. Besides, one of them lived in our house and even though I thanked him, I had experienced what I experienced. I must mention that my older brother was already working there, too.

I eventually took a management position with Good Year Tire and Rubber Company in San Fernando. It gave me an open door to walk away from high school and not look back. Nobody called looking for me to see where I was. Nothing was made of the fact that I was no longer in school, nobody noticed, nobody cared, and I could breathe. I took the retail position because by this time I had lots of retail and customer service experience. My memory of time there is vague, probably because of my drinking and drug use. I don't really remember the years following, either, as I immersed myself in the dark world of cocaine and alcohol.

Using my brother David to make money selling cocaine was easy, as he worked at the auto plant and it was low hanging fruit. Money always seemed to be available, until we started using more and more ourselves. Our lives were overtaken with getting more product to cut, sell, and use.

We would have parties. I say we, but David hosted parties, letting everyone know what was happening and where we lived. That was dangerous. There were more strange and potentially violent characters around and what friends I did have showed up for only one thing - to drink and party, and they knew drugs were available through me and my brother.

David self-destructed behind cocaine, losing his house and everything he owned, eventually going to rehab. I was tired of that life by this time and hadn't worked for a while. Dad showed up now and then. He'd pick me up to go with him, as he worked as a gardener after retirement. I believe he knew what was going on and it was his way of lending support. He would slip me twenty dollars when I helped him, which became weekly.

Becoming a drug addict was not on my road map, but apparently it was on the radar. I didn't see it coming. Or did I? Contradictions followed me around throughout my lifetime. I hated my father's alcoholism, but followed in his footsteps, descending into alcoholism myself. Until the lights came on that fateful night December 6, 1991, when I drove down the highway, drunk yet again after a long night of drinking.

Dad had passed three months earlier on September 6, 1991, and although I didn't feel affected the night he died, I went from the hospital to my mom's house. I will never forget her words and my reaction. She said, "I don't want you boys to start drinking." I have no recollection of saying anything, but the sound of a Miller Light being opened could be heard all through the house when I opened it. I paid no mind to the words of my mother as the old man was gone and the door was open wide for me to step into his drunken footsteps. I was probably drunk every day from September 6th until I was arrested on December 6th.

Going before the judge a month later, on January 3, 1992, I was charged with a DUI and sentenced to twenty-six meetings of Alcoholics Anonymous. It was about 23 days before I surrendered and got sober from alcohol and drugs. Sobriety was not something I ever thought about. Why would I? It was normal to drink and do drugs, at least that's what my life showed me. But here I was, beginning a new and unfamiliar path going forward to I didn't know where.

I did everything the Alcoholics Anonymous people suggested. The number one thing was *not to drink*. I went to meetings, got a sponsor, carried and read the big book, took people that needed rides to meetings and went out for coffee afterwards. My life began to change and I was saying YES to the changes.

When I say my life began to change, I mean the alcohol and drug use part. The rest of my life was a mess and stayed a mess for years to come. I made poor decisions, especially about relationships. Up to this point, I had never really had a serious relationship. I didn't know how. I met women and had sex right out of the gate. In my small mind that was love, although truthfully I didn't know what it was to love. I seemed to pick women that weren't good for me. I started going to church, as single women were abundant there and I was the new guy.

I have to tell you, the women I met in church were just as emotionally unhealthy as I was. They would say yes and even welcome my advances. At times, it was like picking up women in clubs and bars. The women in Alcoholics Anonymous were no different, but possibly even more wounded from what was probably a lifetime of abuse and self-sabotage. I had to be a little careful because I was a newbie and felt like others were watching me. I tended to stay away from the women in Alcoholics Anonymous as sober men and women warned against thirteen stepping in the group.

Thirteen stepping is in reference to the twelve steps of AA, they're the basis of our sobriety. The thirteenth step is in reference to hitting on each other for sex. Sober elders would always warn about this as it could be a threat to one's sobriety. I didn't really know how much I wanted to be sober, because I was doing as suggested and not questioning or thinking about it.

In sobriety, I was engaged more than once and was married three times over a twenty-year period. It wasn't revealed to me until years later why I couldn't maintain a relationship - much less a marriage. It's a strange thing living out loud and getting married more than once in front of friends and family who were mostly Catholic. Later I carried shame about the relationships, which was something I had to face eventually.

I do have to say that none of the women I married were from AA. Two were ladies I met in church and the third I met much later, after my life had taken a dramatic turn. There were no dramatic turns while sitting in AA meetings and having my experience in sobriety. Everything seemed to move painfully slow and sometimes for me even slower. Somehow, I got the message that my life would get better - and it did - but as they say in the big book of AA, sometimes quickly, sometimes slooooooowly. Apparently, I was not in the express lane.

All the jobs I was offered and took were low-level positions at companies where I had no experience. I often had to take the bull by the horns and create a new position for myself. In that way, I created my own experience by answering phones, saying yes, and taking chances. I learned to listen and take things slow, trusting that I could do things that I never learned in school. Overcome with low or no self-esteem, it never occurred to me that saying yes, taking chances, and creating a place for myself was the experience I was having. I had never heard of such a thing until I stepped into my medicine years later.

I worked for my AA sponsor David for a while as an investigator for insurance companies. I spent my days in the car with David or by myself going to courthouses across the counties of Southern California, following the paper trail by pulling and copying files of potential fraudulent claims by individuals. That eventually led to other investigative jobs from other sources. I didn't care for this kind of work, but I was willing to do whatever necessary to maintain an income. I did this until Debbie, a friend from AA, offered me a job as a receptionist at a small tech firm in Los Angeles.

I had never been in front of a computer or even seen one before. When I was hired, the owner James Bradley came in and said, "This is a MAC and this is how you turn it on. If it freezes, unplug it and plug it back in to reboot it. I'm going skiing in Chile for two weeks, if you make a decision and it's wrong, don't worry about it, we'll fix it when I get back." He left, trusting me with his company. I was never given that kind of trust before. My friend Debbie was the in-house accountant and was in the office a couple of times a week. She assured me that I would be fine and over time I was. Trust was something I was never given, so the fresh breath of air felt good on my wounded soul. I hadn't had this feeling of pride since being in that summer school class and learning about the Aztec civilization. I was beaming when I didn't know how to and for the first time in what felt like forever, I was proud of myself.

It wasn't long before I was promoted to become the purchaser/buyer for the company, at times serving as an inside salesman. I realized this was a result of staying sober and saying yes to the unknown without worrying unnecessarily about what could go wrong. This was a new adventure.

Shortly after, I met a woman at church, fell in love, and got married. Kimberly was from Tennessee and experienced the 1994 Northridge earthquake with me. She was frightened out of her mind and when she said she wanted to go back home to Tennessee, I said yes. I mean, that's what husbands do, right? Try to keep their spouse happy.

Willingness seemed to be a big part of my life. Willingness to stay sober, to stay and trust my new position, love my partner, and trust God and myself. I gave my notice at work, packed up everything, and drove across the country to a new beginning. I left everything I knew behind: Mom, family, AA, work, community... everything.

I didn't know it, but I would be driving across the country in a snowstorm. I had never traveled, so had no idea what the weather was like outside of Southern California. By the time we stopped for the night in Williams, Arizona, there was probably a foot of snow on the ground. We stayed overnight and moved on the next morning. I drove until dark and ended that day in Grants, New Mexico. All I remember about Grants was the motels with their neon lights and how inexpensive it was to stay there. We went into a local eatery, full of decorations and run by a strange elderly man. It felt like the kind of a restaurant owned by Fred Sanford of Sanford and Son, the television show. I couldn't wait to eat and get out of there as it felt creepy. I fell asleep that night to the sound of whistles blowing from passing trains and eighteen wheelers moving down highway I-40, which replaced the famous old Route 66.

We arrived three days later in Kimberly's hometown of Morristown, Tennessee, pulling up to her parent's house in the U-Haul with our car in tow. I wasn't sure what I would encounter meeting Kimberly's parents and brothers for the first time. I felt uncomfortably out of place being the only brown person in the house. Kim's parents and brothers seemed to be sweet, but that didn't alleviate my feelings. Her brothers were huge, one six-foot-three and the other six-foot-six. I constantly reminded myself about keeping my place as I was in somebody else's home and it was a long drive back to Los Angeles. Saying that, I didn't know what my place was, as I was a fish out of water trying not to flounder.

The next two years were a strange cultural odyssey and sober experience followed by disappointment, hurt, divorce, and loss. It was a hard time. I made the decision to leave Tennessee, packed up my U-Haul, hitched my car, and headed west, returning home to Los Angeles whooped but not beaten. I was having suicidal thoughts because of my failed marriage. I was driving a company truck thinking, "I could just turn the wheel, drive the truck into a ditch, and nobody would ever know." But I would know and God would know. I just wanted to go home, shame or not. I don't know if that constitutes being a coward, but feeling like I failed really, really hurt my broken heart.

I stayed with my mom until I secured a job and a place to live. Bradley Group hired me back in an instant, although the business had changed in my absence. James Bradley was glad to have me back and I was glad to be back. Truthfully, though, I wasn't fully back. I was an emotional mess and still suicidal.

I immersed myself in AA and church, trying to live a 'normal' life, but it was far from normal. I went to meeting after meeting trying to find relief, but I knew relief would only come with time. It wasn't relief from wanting to drink; the shitty feeling I had inside seemed to dog me day after day. I spoke to my pastors at church about my divorce and the way I was feeling. I also talked to them about the numbers of walking wounded at church who had also gone through divorce and probably needed help as well. I suggested that the church start a divorce recovery class. Pastor Larry looked at me and said, "I'm too busy to take on more, what are you gonna do about it?"

He was right! What was I doing besides sulking and feeling sorry for myself? I was asked to start the divorce recovery program with Assistant Pastor Steve, so we moved forward and made it happen. Creating the group was easier than I thought, and on the first day of the group almost forty people attended. Not all were divorced; some were long time married couples and others simply wanted to support the divorced walking wounded. In any church, divorce and divorcées can be treated like the plague and is almost never talked about outside of gossip.
The pain of my situation began to melt away and I started to feel better just by being proactive in my own life healing. (*Please read that sentence again and soak it in.)

I have to say, starting the divorce recovery group was not just to help myself. I didn't know how to just help myself. I always brought in other people who I felt needed help to make me feel better. I'm saying I didn't know how to mind my own business. They weren't asking for help. It was my way of connecting and I was always looking for connection so I could feel better. I seemed to be a busybody in the process and had to learn over time to mind my own business.

I volunteered to start a new church in the Santa Clarita Valley, in another part of the county. I knew nothing about such things but gave my time anyway. I became the temporary praise leader, leading the new

page 46

congregants in song, setting up church every Sunday, and doing whatever I was asked. It was a small church, so everyone was needed and it was all hands on deck.

I was floating between the divorce recovery group and the new church. At one point, I was asked to make a choice between the two. I chose the new church and moved away from the divorce recovery group. I never knew the fate of the group or whether it continued. My part was done and I felt great about being involved and helping others.

Before leaving the divorce recovery group, I floated between both churches as those and AA provided the only social life I had. One night I went to a dance at the church in Van Nuys, where I met a lovely woman named Astrid from Colombia, South America. She kept looking at me, so I went over and asked her to dance. She said yes. After that night, we decided to go out for a long drive to the mountains in Ventura County. It was a rainy day, but we had fun and took pictures with a disposable camera we picked up at a gas station along the way.

We started seeing each other, even though she was going through a divorce. I was living at my mother's at the time because my grandmother had cancer and Mom was living at her place while taking care of her. Mom asked me to stay at her house so there would be signs of somebody being there, that way nobody would break in. Astrid came over there to spend time with me and we grew closer.

I really had no business seeing Astrid while she was going through the divorce. The thought crossed my mind, but I didn't care. I didn't want to be alone and she was willing to spend time with me. We eventually fell in love and were married and became sextons (caretakers) of a church in Studio City, California where we lived and worked. At the same time, we maintained our presence and responsibilities at Sunshine Christian Church in New Hall, California, the new church where I had volunteered. The Sexton was a position the church gave to an exemplary member who wanted and was willing to take on more than regular church responsibilities. I had become responsible for a church that was open twenty-four hours, making it a safe place for people to come, pray, and find solace. I had held that position as a single man; the church elders trusted me and my judgment.

During our time at the church, Astrid and I tried to have a child. Because we were a bit older, it seemed to be more difficult. She eventually got pregnant and we looked forward to having a child and being a happy family. Astrid was so happy, she jokingly said she wanted to have 10 boys. I was good with one, lol.

Another anniversary of the Sunshine Christian Church came up and the church celebrated with a picnic at a local park. It seemed everybody was invited. I asked Astrid to take it easy, because at this time she was in the early stages of the pregnancy. She just sat on a blanket at the park while the other women and children of the church doted over her. She didn't have to do anything. That changed quickly, as she started having pain in her abdomen. Bleeding, she was helped to the bathroom by the other ladies, then we got in the car and sped off to Urgent Care. It was too late.

Astrid miscarried and we, along with our community, were devastated. This was the hardest thing I ever had to endure, not just my own pain about the loss, but Astrid's pain as well. The grief stayed with us for a long time and getting through it was long and difficult. I couldn't do anything about Astrid's hurt, but I buried myself in AA and church activity trying to kill what I was feeling. Once, to deal with the pain, I booked a room in Las Vegas where we stayed for three days, hiding out and nursing our pain. Then we returned to Los Angeles and reality.

During this time, I felt myself pulling away from Astrid. I only went through the motions of being her husband, I wanted out. I no longer wanted to be married. When we met, I injected myself into her life while she was going through her divorce. I had no business doing so and now I was unhappy in our marriage. I wasn't sure if it was because of the miscarriage or what, but my heart was no longer in the marriage or with Astrid. I told her I wanted a divorce and confessed that I had no business in her life or interrupting her life at the time. This obviously didn't go over well, but after being together for nine years,

I began planning for my departure. She was rightfully angry, but we had to communicate in order to make the upcoming arrangements. I had a close friend named Manny who saw what was going on with me and one day he asked if I had filed for divorce. My response was, "No, I should have the money soon." He asked how much it was, feeling I should get out of where I wasn't happy. I told him how much and he gifted me the money as a path to happiness… Happiness!

My life seemed to go in circles. Apparently, as hard as I tried, I hadn't been happy for a long time. I took a position managing a men's sober living home and moved out of our little church cottage. Even though I was sober myself, I had never managed a sober living home. I lived there for some time, pulling farther and farther away from my marriage.

After the divorce was final, I began dating a woman from my high school who I reconnected with on social media. There are moments of feeling like jumping from the frying pan into the fire and this was exactly the case. Her name was Luz. We were on a date to a local eatery in Northeast Los Angeles and during the conversation she asked, "What would you do if I cheated on you?" Clearly a red flag.

I turned around in the booth we were in, got on my knees, pointed to the back of my head, and said, "Take a good look at the back of my head, because that'd be the last thing you'd see." As much as that bothered me, I ignored it and dated her anyway. Over the course of dating her there were many uncomfortable moments as well as good moments. We talked about life's ups and downs and shared a lot in detail.

Luz was the person who suggested I become a healer after listening to a conversation I was having on the phone with another sober alcoholic. I didn't even know what she was talking about as she suggested that I get trained to become an energy healer. I had to ask, "What is an energy healer?" She explained, "It's like Reiki." "Reiki, what's that?" I had no clue what she was talking about. We had been seeing each other for about a year when she gifted me with an energy healing session with a friend of hers. Let me say right here, right now, me sitting at this keyboard and writing what I write is a direct result of that healing session and the transformation that has been taking place in me ever since.

I was so profoundly affected by that experience, I didn't know what to think. Cathy, the healer who was working on me, held her hands on my feet as the healing session ended. Then I heard her walk by me as she went out the door and down the hall to wash her hands. While she was doing that, I could still feel her holding my feet and I felt glued to the massage table I was laying on. When she reentered the room, I sat up as best I could. It was like somebody had unzipped the front and back of my upper body and I felt fully exposed, like I was wide open. I had never experienced anything like this before.

She had also worked on my kidney area and when she pulled her hands away, I felt physical pain from the stretching of my kidney tissue. How was any of this possible? I never heard of such a thing. She asked me what wolf or dog meant to me, and I responded, "I don't know. Why?" She said a wolf or dog had come into the room during the session and sat down, which left me wondering. At that time, I knew nothing about animal spirits. As we were leaving her office, which was a turn of the century home in the Highland Park area of Los Angeles, I noticed a knocker on the door. It was a wolf. When I mentioned that to Cathy, she said in surprise, "Oh, I never noticed that before."

My life was already starting to transform, and I hadn't even gotten into my car yet. As I drove away, I made a U-Turn to enter the street. When I came to the first stop sign, I saw the strangest thing - a wolf standing in the street right in front of me. I shook my head to clear it, but there it was, a wolf. There are no wolves in Los Angeles, are there?

As I rolled through the intersection, the visual of the wolf started to dissolve and it was actually a Boxer standing behind a parked white van. Were my eyes playing tricks on me? I didn't understand, but I saw what I saw. Cathy's words about dog/wolf were still fresh in my ears. As I was driving home, Luz called and I pulled into a grocery store parking lot to speak with her. She asked how my session was and as I began to answer, I started to cry uncontrollably. She was worried and asked if she should come to where I was. I asked her to just stay on the phone with me. I cried and cried. I was in that parking lot on the phone for almost two hours. When my body calmed down, I drove the rest of the way home with Luz still on the phone. During my session, Cathy had opened me up emotionally. I had never known what it was like to be that vulnerable. I don't remember much about the rest of that night or the following days (daze).

I googled energy healing in the local area and the only thing that came up was a school in Studio City called the "Lionheart Institute of

Transpersonal Healing." I called and made an appointment for the next night to audit a class and get more information.

When I arrived, I met the director of the school and a graduate teacher. There was another lady auditing the class who seemed to be troubled. She talked about feeling suicidal, then she left. I stayed and listened, but honestly wasn't impressed. I later found out that Cathy (the healer who I had a session with) had graduated from that school. When I learned that, I contacted her and talked about my experience. She explained a bit more and not long after, I signed up for classes.

I was given dates, instructions, and the location of where classes were held. When I heard about the location, I was terrified. They were going to be held at the Poverello Retreat Center in San Fernando, California, which in 1966-67 was the Poverello School, the kindergarten I attended and where I was traumatized by abusive nuns.

My first day of classes for energy healing, I stood staring at the same steep driveway that had not changed in all these years. "How am I ever going to do this?" I asked myself. Taking a deep breath, I got back in my car and drove onto the property. It was strange being there after almost fifty years. The main school building made of granite was gone, destroyed during the 1971 Sylmar earthquake. Everything else looked the same except for hedges surrounding a fountain that replaced the old school building.

Despite my fear and apprehension being back on that property, I knew returning to that place would be powerful for me. I mean, how many people get to go back to ground zero and learn to heal and serve from their past traumas? I found the room where we were meeting. The class was full. I felt a little out of place because of my age and lack of knowledge. We were asked to introduce ourselves in front of the teaching staff and students.

There were approximately thirty-four students there on my first day. When it was my turn, I stood and introduced myself. I shared about going to school on that same property almost fifty years prior as a child. The class was kind of blown away by that. I told them about the abuse I had suffered at the hands of the nuns back then. I shared about my healing experience with Cathy, who was in the room as a teacher. Then I shared about how my father was an alcoholic, living with heart disease, lung, and liver cancer before he passed and how I didn't want to die that way. I explained that I was diabetic and wanted to heal the diabetes living in my second and third chakras from low self-esteem and the broken connections in my family.

After the introductions, we took a break. One of the other students said to me, "You can't choose how you're gonna die." And I responded, "No, but I can choose how I'm *not* gonna die. I don't have to die like my father." One of the teachers, Doctor Piam Hakimi, an Eastern/Western medical doctor, took me aside and asked where I learned about the chakras. I responded, "I don't know anything about chakras, why?" With a surprised look, he asked, "So how do you know to attribute your diabetes to the second and third chakras?" I just looked at him, saying, "I didn't know, I just spoke what intuitively came out of my mouth." I was already delving deep into my intuition without realizing it. Dr. Hakimi intended to teach the chakra system over the next two days and was really surprised by what I said. In hindsight, I was already channeling information from the spirit world of which I knew nothing about, but it became a part of my everyday life and being from that point on.

During a break, I took time by myself to walk around the campus in silence, taking in the present and past. I was walking along the outer hedge that surrounded the fountain when I came upon a Red-Tailed Hawk, one of several that lived in the palm trees on the property. As I rounded a curve, there she was, standing in the grass looking at me. I stopped and stood still, simply taking in its presence. We stared at each other for what seemed like quite some time. Then I spoke, thanking her for being with me. She turned, hopped off, and flew into the trees. I was amazed. I never had such an experience, nor did I know what it meant. As I turned to walk back to class, I noticed a hawk feather on the grass and thought to myself, "She left me a gift!" To this day, I still have and cherish that feather. I returned to class but shared nothing about what I had experienced.

Energy healing was taught to us using the Barbara Brennan method, based on an Indian or Chinese method of moving Qi/Prana (energy) in the body. I was amazed at how quickly I caught on to moving energies and how I felt them differently than other students. In class we would practice our new-found skills on each other. I loved having the other students work on me, it was such an amazing time.

Students talked about seeing old weapons, chains, and things in the place of so-called wounds of people they were working on. They explained that those wounds were the 'why' of people who had issues in their tissues or blocks in the emotional body.

We did an exercise with one of the teachers to be able to see our spirit guides. He had us sit in a circle and asked if we had any physical issues to share. The person I was partnered with said he had an injury to his right shoulder. I was asked to place my left hand on his shoulder and my right hand on his hand, allowing the energy to flow from my hand to his injured shoulder while keeping my eyes closed and not forcing anything to happen. We were asked what we could see.

To my amazement, in my mind's eye I saw my arm as a tube of bright sea-blue water moving into my partner's shoulder. I could see a boy swimming through the tube of water. He was darked skinned, had longish bushy brown hair, and wore a loincloth. As a matter of fact, he looked exactly like "Mowgli" from the Jungle Book animated movie. Wow, what an experience, even if what I was seeing wasn't really what I was seeing. The boy I saw was actually a familiar representation of who and what my spirit guide really is. I named my spirit guide Mowgli because I didn't know his real name. I didn't need to. At least, that's what I believed and understood from him almost instantly. My spirit guide (Mowgli) was a huge, ancient, almost rock looking man, about seven or eight feet tall. He seemed to be a dark-skinned indigenous or native who I refer to as the Chief. I didn't say a lot in the class about this as I felt it was strictly for me and none of anyone else's business.

After that, when I experienced Mowgli, I experienced him as a feeling. When I did see him, he was sometimes wearing a buckskin shirt, pants, moccasins, and a large war bonnet headdress. Other times, he was almost solid rock wearing a loincloth. I understood and understand him to be an ancient, as I believe I am. Where did I get the idea that I was ancient? That idea came from the things I was saying, doing, and teaching. Outside of the energy healing school, I was never taught in this lifetime how to do the things I was doing. Where did the wisdom coming out of my mouth come from? I surprised myself at nearly every turn and word I uttered. Quotes poured out of me. As I sat quietly after waking up in the morning, I listened and my guides gave me information in the form of quotes to share.

One of the biggest things I experienced while at Lionheart Transformational Transpersonal Energy Healing was offering healing sessions at Christmas for the nuns who still lived on the property, one of which was there in 1967, when I attended as a child. My willingness to do healing sessions on them spoke volumes as to how far I had come since my first day in class holding hate and disdain for the nuns even after almost fifty years. That all seemed to be gone and I was able to offer myself to them on that healing day.

I received my certificate of completion for the hours necessary to become a healer. I had also become an audio-video person while I was involved with the school and my time was coming to an end, both as a student and as an audio-video volunteer.

While I was assisting with the audio-video portion, every now and again I would step in and assist with classes, making suggestions or adjusting the posture of new students. At one point, I was approached by Laura, the director of Lionheart, and told not to touch students, that I didn't know what I was doing. I looked at her and asked, "Well, what did I pay tuition for?"

Not long after, she approached me and said, "We need more male teachers at Lionheart and think you would be an excellent teacher. But you will have to take a class to become certified as a counselor." However, that class was about $9,000.00 and I didn't have that kind of money. I asked her, "What do I need to take this for? I'm already teaching." I told her I was more interested in shamanism and declined. When I used the word shamanism, I didn't really know what it meant, but it came out of my mouth. The universe obviously heard me because my life started to change once again.

While I was in the energy healing school, I started reading a book Luz had given me for my birthday, "It Calls You Back" by author Luis J. Rodriguez. Within the pages of this book, I found similarities aside from our last names. So much so that I couldn't put the book down. My hunger for reading at that time was so fierce I would buy books and sometimes read them two or three times. I read that Luis and I had lived in some of the same places and walked the same streets of Los Angeles.

At the time, I was living in an older part of Los Angeles called Highland Park, an enclave of hillside homes in an old Mexican neighborhood full of hipsters, gangsters, musicians, and artists. The train from downtown Los Angeles to Pasadena and beyond ran through it. There, I was introduced to friends who played in bands. I had always wanted to play in a band and one day my friend Chris invited me to Whittier to check out an Afrobeat Orchestra he played bass in. I went and took along my old alto saxophone, which I hadn't played for over thirty years. While I was there, I took out my horn and started to play with the band. At the end of the evening, I was invited by the band leader to join them. I took the opportunity and said yes. He liked the way I interacted with the other musicians and wasn't afraid, even after I hadn't played for so many years, to take a chance with me.

At the same time, I found through his book that Luis Rodriguez had lived in San Fernando and was married to a lady named Trini. She owned Tia Chuchas, a cultural center and bookstore in Sylmar, not far from where he lived. His wife was the sister of a now congressman I went to high school with in San Fernando. Luis also talked about doing Sweat Lodge in San Fernando, which made my ears stand up. Wow! Sweat Lodges! I had never done such a thing. In his book he tells how the cultural center was a direct link to the sweat lodge, so I went there and asked about it. They gave me the name and phone number of an elder at the sweat named Picos. I called Picos, and he asked why I wanted to go. I explained where I was at in my life and he invited me to come. Not everybody was welcome to participate in sweats and I was willing to do anything to have the experience.

San Fernando, the place of my birth, was becoming central to the transformation I was beginning to experience. I had completed healing school and now played in an East L.A. band, a lifelong dream. I didn't realize it at the time, but the sweat lodge would change my life, opening the doorways of my spiritual future and connecting with my deeper indigenous nature and family lineage.

As I established my healing practice, I invited people to have sessions in my home. I was to do nineteen healings to receive my final certification. I completed them and was soon welcoming paying clients, some that remain my friends to this day. I became a deeper part of the cultural community as I stepped into my medicine and continued playing in the band. Another opportunity appeared, and I began crafting Christmas ornaments from Dia de Los Muertos (Day of the Dead) materials.

I became more known and even popular, meeting people who encouraged me in all aspects of music, art, and my healing practice. I was playing night clubs and festivals and started selling my art privately and publicly. This new-found love for treasures that were becoming more and more prevalent in my life were happening because of saying YES to myself after a lifetime of no. I always felt I had to do what others wanted or expected me to do, and here I was at the crossroads of my life, a fifty something year old apparently beginning a new life.

Eventually, I grew tired of Luz insulting me and using her education to do so. She was a social worker with a BA and seemed to constantly look down her nose at me, making comments because the healing practice wasn't developing like she felt it should. However, I will say I did go back to school to get my GED as I had dropped out of high school, something I never talked about.

I studied for the GED and went to classes at an adult school in Chinatown. I tested and scored an 87%. I was proud of that as I had never been a good student. I probably could have lived the rest of my life without the GED, but I'm grateful for the accomplishment after so many years. Luz was the inspiration for much of what I was doing, but I hated being talked down to by the elitist she showed herself to be. It was not long after that I stopped seeing her and sought out a different kind of happiness with regard to relationships.

I attended my first sweat lodge, inviting my friend Carlos who was a defense attorney I met at a local coffee house in my neighborhood. We hit it off during our first conversation. He had just arrived back in the country from mountain climbing in Kenya. As we talked, he began to tell me about his experiences in Kenya but stopped himself as tears came to his eyes. He asked if he could tell me about it another time, over morning coffee at a different place. Apparently, his experience was so powerful he wanted to share it in a more private and less vulnerable setting. Carlos seemed to be a sensitive person in an attorney's body and mind. The coffee house where we met was full of tattooed men who worked in TV and film, artists, mechanics, and MMA fighters. It wasn't the place to have a sensitive conversation.

Carlos and I became not only friends, but he was one of my first long term clients and became a trusted brother. One day, he met me in San Fernando for a late lunch and then we headed to the location of the sweat lodge, where we met Picos in person. I also met Hector, Papa Luz, and Armando who were the elders of that particular ceremonial lodge. It was explained that when we go to a lodge, we bring a tobacco offering, water, a covered dish of food to share, and a donation of some sort. It was also explained that we come early for fellowship, to chop wood, prepare the lodge, and help with anything else that needed to be done for the ceremony.

It was an honor to be there and to meet these men who would lead us into a different way of being, the way of our ancestors. The time came to line up with other men, but we didn't just line up, we lined up according to where the elder Hector placed us in line. This was something he did by listening to spirit.

We were smudged with sacred sage and ushered into the lodge (*inippi* as it is known by the Lakota). I came out during the second round, as I couldn't take the heat and breathing was difficult. Papa Luz came out behind me and said it was okay to come out, but I was to cut back on sugar and other things I was eating. I took this to heart, went back inside, and stayed for the rest of the ceremony. I was glad Papa Luz took the time with me. Men had never taken time with me in that way.

In hindsight, it was the same kind of time I was taking with Carlos but hadn't realized it. My relationships with men were starting to change and become more personal. In AA, my relationships were only about sobriety - or so it felt. I was now part of a healing community, a ceremonial lodge, an all-male Afrobeat orchestra, and fellowshipping with men on a regular basis nearly every morning. My world was looking different. I wasn't excluding women from my life; life was just taking me to the places I needed to learn from at the time.

The women who were a part of the ceremonial sweat lodge didn't sweat with the men, as women should be allowed to speak of things personal to them in an open way without potential threat from males. Women had issues unique and personal to them, and men did not need to be privy to those things. This is probably a strange thing to hear in times of equality, but the safety and well-being of the women was of utmost importance to us. The women did come from time to time to support us by bringing food and fellowship outside the lodge and the men would support the women with the building and keeping of the sacred fire while they were in ceremony.

I was taught about the four directions, the medicine wheel, and the elements by my elders and other men. When I heard what they had to share, I started spending more time outdoors to listen and watch for messages and omens. I began to receive from the sky, the trees, water, fire, land, and animals.

During this time, one of my clients introduced me to a woman who was to become my closest ally in my transformation. Kikey, who was an actress, had been coming to me for help for quite some time. She told me about her friend Emma, a massage therapist and a shaman. I instantly felt I had to meet her. We were introduced via Facebook. Emma and her daughter Victoria were partners in a healing studio called Que Linda Boutique/Body and Soul Studios in La Crescenta. One morning, through Facebook, I learned there was an event about third eye intuition with Michael Brenner that day. I jumped in my car and made my way to the studio. When I walked in, I was greeted with a big voice saying "Manos de Luz!"

In front of me was a beautiful silver haired woman, looking like a shaman would probably look. She put her hand out to shake mine and greet me. The instant our hands touched, I felt electricity or energy move up my arm from her hand. Manos de Luz is what I called myself in business at the time and that's what Emma knew me by. Wow! This was more than I could imagine, but here I was, in front of Emma Molina-Ynequez. I sat down and tried to be present for Michael Benners' talk. In truth, all I wanted to do was talk with Emma. I already knew I wanted to learn from her. I had re-become the hungry child inside of me and was willing to listen and learn. I found my willingness was the biggest thing I could come into.

After that event, I dropped by the studio from time to time or called Emma to visit and have coffee or lunch. We would meet at a local nature reserve called Descanso Gardens and take long walks. Emma shared her wisdom on healing, relationships, and spirituality. We talked on many subjects and there was always something to learn. Those walks were important in my early days, I appreciated someone talking directly with me, making me feel important for the first time in my life.

It did wonders for my soul and my heart. It gave me hope and something to look forward to. Emma and I became closer friends over time. I don't believe I could have had intimate talks like those with friends other than Carlos, Emma, and Stormie.

I was dating a beautiful woman named Stormie, an artist who lived in my neighborhood. It was another heart-opening opportunity, as we became friends and lovers based on art, food, and each of our indigenous natures. She was slender with long black hair and beautiful brown skin. She was the kind of woman I always imagined I would be with. Stormie loved that I was in the band and on my path as a healer, learning indigenous ways of medicine and ceremony. We would get together at the Rose Bowl and walk her dogs around the 3.5-mile path. Our conversations were similar to ones I had with Emma, but with romance added to the mix. She came to my gigs, never complaining about who or what I was. She gave me gifts that were meaningful to my new life path. Our relationship wasn't totally based on sex, even though it was a part of the relationship. We were more kindred spirits who got along well.

One day, Stormie called and mentioned that Sara Eagle Woman needed a drummer for her Spirit Circles, held once a month at the Golden Bridge Yoga studio in Hollywood. I had never experienced a spirit circle and never heard of Sara Eagle Woman, but I said yes to Stormie and showed up for the event. I had already started making drums (or should say I made my first drum), so I took it with me along with some shakers and rattles I used in the band. When I arrived, there was a powwow drum there for me to play, along with what I brought. I had never played or drummed in this way and was introduced to a whole new world in just one night. A sacred circle was marked on the floor with the opening to the direction of the east, the place of fire where Grandfather Sun rises. When attendees wanted to enter the circle, it is traditional to enter and exit through the opening in the east. The attendees were smudged and escorted to their seats around the perimeter of the sacred circle.

I have to admit, I didn't know what I was doing. But I showed up for Stormie, Sara Eagle Woman, and myself. The second time I drummed for the spirit circle, I showed up with a bit more confidence and was ready for the ceremony. Even though I didn't understand this as a ceremony, I was learning to be in ceremony any time I was playing a rattle or a drum. I drummed and danced for three hours. By this time, I learned the spirits love it when we drum and sing, but they really love it when we dance. So, at every opportunity, I was drumming and dancing, whether alone or in groups.

The third time I drummed for Sara Eagle Woman's spirit circle, I took a chance, picked up the powwow drum and stepped into the sacred circle to drum while all were dancing. What an amazing experience! The participants began dancing around the drum as I was moving, drumming, and dancing, through the circle.

As I was dancing and drumming, I began to feel my body ascend. Moving upward, I felt like I was moving through clouds, mist, and light, then the skies opened and everything got dark, star-filled, and quiet. I was standing in front of who I believe to be Great Spirit. The air and everything around me felt soft, warm, and comfortable, as if I was being held by my mother. Even the silence gave me that safe, warm feeling. Great Spirit looked at me and said, "You, your voice, hands, drum, mallet, and heart are ONE." I didn't get a chance to say anything, and before I knew it, I was making my way back down and back into the sacred circle. There everyone was still dancing without missing a beat.

I believe Great Spirit had given me my life's charge and what I was to do with the medicine given. By medicine I mean making, playing, and singing, using the drum to carry Great Spirit and the messages of the ancient ones. They wanted me to share what I was given with whomever would listen. This feeling came over me as I drummed and I couldn't stop crying. Wow! Did I imagine this? Did it really happen?

It was all too real, seeing and meeting Great Spirit. I never thought that I could experience anything like this. I mean, God is depicted as an intense man with long white hair and beard and a white robe, the Almighty in the Sistine Chapel in Rome. What I experienced here was gentleness and kindness, direct but safe and comfortable.

When the spirit circle ended, I was soaking wet from drumming and dancing. What a feeling! What an experience! How could I explain my experience to others? Maybe I should keep it to myself. At the end of all the spirit circles, the participants line up, are anointed with oil, and given a blessing by Sara Eagle Woman. I was asked to get in line by

Sara's apprentices. When it was my turn, Sara said to me, "What did you bring back into the circle? You brought back giants?" She anointed me and then blew into my chest. With my eyes closed, I could see and feel her breath penetrate my chest. I had only experienced this once before, during a soul retrieval with Amanda Foulger, a shaman I met in California as I was beginning my journey.

It was obvious to me that Sara Eagle Woman had seen my spirit ascend. These experiences accelerated my spiritual life. I made myself available monthly for her spirit circles from that point forward. At the same time, I was attending sweat lodge and doing everything I could to change things in my life.

I attended men's circles where we read from the Four Agreements by Don Miguel Ruiz and shared about our individual experiences with the Toltec teachings. I had already been reading this book and others like it and was steeping myself in the soul teachings they offered. I read these books over and over again; when I finished, I went back to the beginning and read them again. I have talked with people who tell me they've read these books as well, but it was obvious they simply read the words.

My intent was not just to read for head knowledge, but to put these teachings into practice. I wanted to become new in my life by moving away from the things my life had taught me previously. I started talking about the pain, shame, wounds, and trauma in my life and began transforming those things into a new way of being. This was what I wasn't getting from Alcoholics Anonymous. By now, I knew sobriety. Continuing to sit on my hands was not going to change the same old tired life of religious beliefs and what I was starting to view as false teachings.

I began to view the spiritual world through the eyes of my heart and started to soften. I was able to share things on a deeper level and as I shared, I released from my emotional body and my physical body began to transform. At that time, I weighed 238 lbs. After I started at Lionheart and because of the things I was willing to do, my physical body began to change. I was willing to purge the old self and my suffering, and my body transformed from an obese 238 lbs. to 160 lbs. in just months. I worked to give myself things that were better, different, and good for me after a lifetime of toxicity. I was willing to say *yes* to myself after a lifetime of no. I never felt I was good enough or worthy enough to be more, do more, love more. Where would I learn that? It's not taught in schools and my early home life didn't teach me anything but how to be a failure.

The more I was willing to listen to spirit and be in silence, the more I heard differently. I received direction which I knew was true. I would walk with Emma and listen to her wisdom teachings. She wholeheartedly listened to what I had to say, which I had not experienced before. I started feeling validated and in fact WAS validated. This was something I wrestled with as I had gone through life without validation and wanted to drink from that cup. So, from that cup I drank and deeper I went.

I was introduced and invited to attend Hindi teachings by Swamis. At first, I was uncomfortable going because I didn't know most of the attendees, but soon made friends and started to find and feel my comfort zone. I learned to sing kirtan in languages I didn't understand but was willing to try anyway. They served food afterwards and I was trying foods I had never heard of or seen before. Again, I was saying *yes* after a lifetime of self-judgment and saying no to myself. Instead of thoughts like, "Those are weird people, that is strange food," I moved away from judgmental thoughts and feelings about unfamiliar things. I opened myself to the blessings given and was gifted by the decision to say YES.

I made friends with Swami Nikhilanand Ji, who taught and led kirtan from time to time at Lionheart, the Temple, or at private residences where I attended for his teachings. One day I called him to ask if he would like to go on a hike and he said yes. I was a bit surprised at his response as I would never think of asking a priest or minister to go on a hike. Because of my upbringing, there was always distance between those types and their flock of congregants. But Swami was different. I picked him up at the temple and he was ready, wearing his orange robe, hiking shoes, and a ball cap. We drove up to Topanga State Park, in the mountains that separate the San Fernando Valley and Malibu on the Pacific Ocean. We made our way to the top of a mountain, hiking in the warm afternoon. At first, I felt strange hiking with a Swami. Who was I to have this experience? I was almost embarrassed and felt unworthy, but again, here I was saying *yes*.

We chatted the whole time. I don't even remember what we talked about, which makes me laugh now. We didn't have to talk about anything, looking back on it. We were there for the natural beauty and the experience of hiking in nature. We hiked to the top of a mountain where we sat and just took in the beauty of the surrounding area. I even took a picture of Swami standing on the peak of that mountain dressed in his orange robe and ball cap with the beautiful blue sky as the backdrop. Appropriate for the Swami. We eventually made our way back to the car to go for lunch. As I drove, I looked for an Indian restaurant as I wanted to honor Swami with food he might be accustomed to eating. I found great pleasure spending time with this amazing teacher. He never at any time tried to sell me on Hinduism or any aspects of religion. Swami was a beautiful, gentle soul and I appreciated him greatly. He and other Swami teachers taught me that God or Krishna was simply bliss. Gosh it was so easy, no hell fire and brimstone.

Discomfort still bubbled up every time I had a new experience. I had been alcohol and drug free for almost twenty years but was still bristling from fear of being found out, being a fraud, being stupid. I felt like I put myself in positions of employment where I was in over my head. I worked in technology, selling computers and components for film and video editing systems. I worked as an inside salesman and procurement officer and buyer, which I was pretty good at, but was never comfortable with learning more or accelerating in my knowledge of technology and what I could accomplish.

Even writing this, I never felt smart enough and sometimes still feel like "Why should I waste my time? Who would read what I write?" I was existing in the darkness with my feelings and self-esteem but didn't know how to find a way out.

I didn't realize it, but I was actually finding my way out. I began making drums and selling them at the same time I was seeing clients and strengthening my healing muscle. I drummed for Sara Eagle Woman and went to sweat lodge ceremony monthly. I was playing in the mighty Mexico68 Afrobeat Orchestra, working in technology, and assisting at Lionheart.

My life was full and busy and I was living out loud. My inner worlds were beginning to overlap each other. My friend Carlos was going to sweat lodge and Sara Eagle Woman's spirit circles with me. One of my elders came to hear and support me and my band. I met a beautiful woman at Lionheart and Lionheart students became interested in the drums I was making. The owner of the company I worked for sometimes called me early in the morning to ask me if I would smudge the office. I also participated in the first of many healing events at the Que Linda Boutique/BodyNSoul Studio with Emma and her daughter Victoria.

Smudging became a big part of my practice as I hiked in the mountains and canyons to harvest what I needed instead of using store-bought sage. When hiking, I was guided to touch, feel, smell, and taste plants and started learning about basic plant medicines. I use the word guided, as I knew nothing about such things. Because I was willing, things were opening up for me in a big way. I'd be walking with Emma and something would call to me from the plants and the trees. I began to see portals everywhere I looked, passageways to the spirit world. I would see fairies and leprechauns in the bushes close to the ground. I would disappear into the bushes while walking with Emma and find mushrooms and plants that I spent time with while Emma waited. She, more than anyone, understood what was happening to me.

Emma and I spent our sacred time together walking at Descanso gardens, where the blue herons and owls lived. One day as we walked and talked, I saw feathers - a lot of them - and began picking them up. I learned they were Owl feathers. I also found and picked up beautiful Blue Heron feathers, which I have to this day. We even had an encounter with Deer on that property. Deer eventually became one of my first medicine/spirit animals. While we walked, we saw an Oak Tree surrounded by small mirrors and we both wondered what the idea was. The answer was given to me almost as fast as I wondered what I was seeing.

The spirit guides told me, "This is a Grandmother (tree). She sees and experiences everything around her, the sky, clouds, the sun and moon, birds of the air, ground animals, plants, trees, and you and me. She sees all things except herself, she gives and gives and never asks in return. Grandmother tree is truly selfless and only gives." Spirit was giving me my first big lesson. I looked at my life and said, "I am the tree that wasn't knocked down by the four winds. I am still standing. I am rooted and fruited and I raise my branches to the heavens. The birds of the air rest in my branches and eat of my fruit. And what is my fruit? My fruit is the experiences I share of how I got from point A to point B, that's it and that's all."

Wow! Did this really come out of my mouth, did the spirits really say this to me and for me? They most certainly did! Whenever I led an event, had a client, or was speaking in a teaching capacity I shared this with all that would listen. Emma's influence was becoming noticeable, and I am proud to say she was my teacher. There were others who wanted to step up to teach me what they do. With some, I found myself not resonating with what they were trying to teach, I felt like it was forced and not coming naturally. One teacher said she was a shaman, but I only heard dark and egoic information come from her mouth. Emma wasn't like that; she was kind and her wisdom did not feel like it was ego based. The other person acted like she wanted me to know about her, she wanted to teach me more. I didn't feel any love from her or caring for me, she only wanted to teach me what I felt was hocus pocus magic. I wasn't interested.

Love and loving energy were becoming part of me, feeling and giving love to others without expectation. Not the romantic love we were taught to strive for or express for others on Valentine's Day. I was learning from Emma that love was the place where everything I did flowed from. Whenever I put my healing hands on somebody or worked with a group, love was primary. Not just love for them, but the utmost love and care for myself. Lionheart was also teaching me to love from a healing place, a healing of the self and a place of self-care, healing the wounded soul. I believe there are things that you can't force, but rather allow love to flow in and through.

I knew nothing about self-care before I became a healer. It was never part of my thoughts or vocabulary. Self-care? What was that? After a while I began to understand what happened to me as a child and the deep wounds I carried. It was obvious I had to make changes in my life. I could no longer carry resentment towards those who treated me the way they did. AA talked about that in its own way, which kept me from drinking. But energy healing, sweat lodge, Emma, my elders, and the spirit world were speaking to me and asking me to look at my life in a different way. I realized I had to forgive the wounded child and all who I felt wronged me. The soul retrieval I did with Amanda Foulger was especially powerful because she gave me specific instructions of what I was to do. I not only listened to her, but I also did what she asked me to do, and it changed my life in the most amazing way.

I began to understand where I needed to forgive and started to understand the wounded child within. I began giving the wounded child what was necessary for my healing and growth. I started using the Ho'oponopono to heal myself. The Ho'oponopono is a healing prayer from Hawaii of forgiveness for self and others. I started to understand how I was a splintered soul from the lifelong hurts that I had been carrying as a child. I learned I had to go back and rescue that child to integrate the child with the man. I started to understand that the wounded child had no ability to grow from where the wounds had happened.

As the healing process progressed, I discovered integration was an important part of the rescue. I needed to give the broken child the love, care, and understanding that I had not received as a child. I needed to pick that child up from when he was five years old. I like to say the child was holding his arms out to be picked up by the one who loved him most. I gave that child what he needed to heal. I had the understanding that the child was no longer in real time and needed healing and care as he was as an adult, so I gave myself what the man needed to heal. I gave myself things like naps, good food, healthier relationships, friendships with groups of men, daily hikes, and whatever self-care I needed to heal myself. I did things that I hadn't done before.

I became an artist and started using my photography to make greeting cards and Day of the Dead ornaments, selling them privately and at art fairs and different community events. I became somewhat well known for what I was doing as a healer, drum maker, musician, and artist which brought me much happiness while healing the little boy at the same time. When I was in the band, I arrived at the venues early to smudge and clear the space to change the energy. I was nurturing the nature of who I was, what I was, and who I had always been. I didn't know the word or meaning of the word nurture until spirit told me what it was. As I healed and nurtured myself, it became a big part of my vocabulary and the conversation when sharing with others. I started talking about picking up the little boy who cried "Uppy Uppy" as he held his arms up to be picked up and held with love.

I learned I wasn't the only one who wanted and needed to be picked up and hugged after a lifetime of hurt, wounds, shame, trauma, and pain. With clients, I could see these emotions stuck in their bodies as dis-ease or disease. Cancers, migraines, obesity, drinking, drugs, overeating, low self-esteem, anger, and fear would show up as not healed. As I brought up uncomfortable subjects, clients experienced relief as these things were no longer burdening them as their big secret. I could speak to them because of my own healing and deep work. I began recommending certain practices they could follow, to finally experience letting go and deep healing.

I began seeing and experiencing the guides, spirits, spirit animals, past pets, relatives, people, and experiences that lived in the memory of the body and the soul. I asked clients about these things and sometimes (or most of the time) they were unaware of these kinds of memories. This became an important part of their healing and understanding. I was learning to do soul retrieval through conversations and the asking of the uncomfortable questions., taking clients back to that place where they were splintered from themselves. Then we would move to the table for the hands-on healing. This was directed by my intuitive nature and the spirit guides.

Through this time, I was meeting many healers of different modalities and created a group called The Healers Tribe. The idea was that we would have a collective of healers available for whatever healing a person wanted or needed. The first meeting of the collective Healers Tribe included fifty-four healers. We sat in a huge circle. You could look across the spokes of what made up this wheel of healers and see the different modalities across the room. Around the circle, each healer shared about who they were and what they offered.

After several months, I married Vanessa, the woman I met at Lionheart. We began a life together which was sadly short lived. We were married for two years and she became a part of the healing events I was doing. As we worked together, she brought a whole new understanding for me of the hurts and wounds women carry, especially from molestation as young girls. I learned how to ask my female clients about those situations without feeling threatening to them. I remember hearing Vanesa talk at an event with twenty-four women about her own molestation. She said, "What you should know and understand is the molestation is no longer happening, so you no longer have to carry it in your body." Wow! This realization was mind blowing to me. It didn't mean that they didn't have to do any further healing work, it meant they could understand where to start.

At the first meeting of The Healers Tribe, I noticed something interesting. As the meeting went on, Vanessa started coughing and excused herself from the room several times as it became more distracting. To me, when somebody coughs it comes from a heart issue, whether heart, lungs, or air as "I love, I am loved, or I don't have the capacity to love or be loved." This was understanding the broken heart in an interesting way. Vanessa often came to my drum journeying events but would exit right away afterward to sit in the car while I pressed the flesh and packed up my drums and medicine tools.

People began noticing when she wasn't in the room and started asking what was going on. That night, her coughing at the Tribe Wellness meeting turned out to be bilateral pulmonary pneumonia that lasted for months. More than once, I believed I was going to lose her. I was half right, she didn't die, but her love did. It became obvious we wouldn't be together much longer. Her broken heart or lack of love showed itself through the pneumonia.

I wasn't sure how to feel. I took her to doctor appointments, fearing the worst for her. I didn't know how to handle it. I was let go from my job, but didn't want to go back to that kind of work life. She wanted me to get a job. I wanted to work more as a healer, seeing clients and building my healing practice. It was obvious she didn't want that for me but wanted me to seek solid employment. I was unhappy and started feeling resentful about her being sick and not supporting me. Maybe I was being selfish. Or was I just conflicted? I would get angry and mumble things under my breath, sometimes doing it out loud where she could hear me.

Vanessa slowly got better, and I finally took a part-time job at a natural health food store. I was not happy and neither was she, but I thought it would buy me time. Vanessa was less than happy as a friend of hers had lent her money for us to live on and pay rent while she was sick. I started feeling uncomfortable at home and it became obvious our marriage was ending. And it did.

We were supposed to go to a family reunion for her side of the family, but both of us were uncomfortable with the idea of going together. On the day she left with her adult children for the reunion, I came home and the locks on the doors had been changed. I was upset and slid a window next to the door open, reached in, and unlocked the door. I called her to let her know I was in the house. She promptly turned around and came back. I assured her I would cause no problems and she reluctantly left with me staying at the house.

I had been renting a healing space in a turn of the century home in Altadena, not far from the house. While she was gone, I arranged to rent a small bedroom just across the hall from my office space. When she returned, I was out of the house and making strides to move forward. She filed for divorce and asked when I could sign the divorce papers. Where I had to go to sign them was close by, but I was not happy about doing it. I told her I would sign them on February 14, Valentine's Day. I was being mean and spiteful and when I showed up to sign, I let my anger be known. I had so much to learn about myself in that way.

Looking back, I feel bad for what I put Vanessa through emotionally. I finally realized that I didn't have any business being in a relationship because I didn't know how to be in one. After the divorce, sometimes we would get together for coffee. I always seemed to get angry then, making snide and rude remarks. We eventually stopped getting together as I didn't even know how to do that in a loving way. I wanted to talk and say I was sorry but couldn't - I just didn't know how. I was a long way from being healed and I had a long way to go.

While I was involved with the Healers Tribe and Roots for Wellness Studio in Sierra Madre, the owner Amy and I created and birthed a healing arts fair with the owner of the studio. I brought together forty-five healers and vendors to facilitate a day of healing with people from all over Los Angeles. We used the parking lot for most of the event and the studio to showcase different healers and modalities. We offered each healer a free half hour to teach, conduct sound healings, lead meditations, or whatever forms of healing they offered. It was a complete success, and everyone was happy with the results. I seemed to have my fingers in many pies and wasn't afraid to try something new.

One of the great things coming out of the Healing Arts Fair was meeting Master Sio, a healer of extraordinary proportions. We got together for lunch every couple of weeks. He was from New Zealand and had lived in silence with the shamans on the island of Oahu before coming to Los Angeles. My relationship with Master Sio eventually became a bone of contention in my marriage to Vanessa. As I was teaching myself (or I should say the guides and spirits were teaching me) to take people on a journey with the drum, I practiced with Vanessa. She would share her experiences with me after our home sessions and the studio sessions with others.

One day I took Vanessa on a journey. She laid on the couch, with me drumming at her feet for about twenty minutes. When I finished, I used my hands to scan her energetic field. As I did, her body jumped. When she came back into the room after her journey, she asked me why I was so rough with my hands, because she knew me to have a very soft touch. I explained that I never placed my hands physically on her. She said it felt like she was laying on a giant tiger and she could hear and feel it purr, she could feel its fur as it moved underneath her. She told me that she saw a shaman holding a stick and hitting the floor with it, and heard the word Haka. I knew that Haka was a ceremonial Māori war dance challenge in New Zealand, usually performed in groups representing a tribe's pride. I had no idea what this meant at the time, but after I met Master Sio it became clear.

One day Master Sio called and invited me to lunch. Vanessa asked why he didn't want to meet with her and I said he didn't invite her to come. She was upset, stating that she had seen him on her journeys several times, that he had to be here for her. I explained that not all the things we experience during a journey are for us. Sometimes, the things we experience are for others. I believed it was a case of that. Over the weeks, months and years, Master Sio met friends and contemporaries in the spiritual healing community. Vanessa and I slowly drifted apart and eventually divorced.

Chapter 8: Nurturing Your Nature

My healing journey continued as I developed strong, long-lasting relationships and did more of the things I didn't know how to do before. There was a lot happening to and for me. I was paying attention to signs and omens and began to see and notice things I had never even thought of before. The relationship with my elders at the ceremonial lodge became pivotal as I was more willing to allow myself to be vulnerable to the teachings and care of others. Whenever they gathered outside the lodge, I made myself available as I never knew what I would learn.

Emma, Master Sio, Marsh Engle, Mystic Jeanne Love, and the teachings of the Gita were all heavy influences for me. I was reading spiritual and self-help books as if I was starving. I listened to teachers like Dr. Gabor Mate who seemed to talk and believe as I did, lending his confirmation to the things the spirit world was saying to me. I even went to hear him speak and learned more about where I came from and what was my "Why."

I was obsessed with my Why. In Alcoholics Anonymous, I learned about the causes and conditions of my alcoholism, but that only scratched the surface. As much as AA helped me, it fell short in other areas. AA taught me that I suffer from a spiritual malady, but I felt like I couldn't get past a certain barrier in the meetings. It felt limiting. I was beginning to trust myself more and more, feeling and listening to my intuition. I started living in trust, even though I never felt trustworthy. I didn't realize I could be trustworthy. I paid attention to giving myself - the little Anthony me, the big Anthony me, and the Walking Crow me - more of what he'd always wanted and needed.

I literally began to trust myself so much I felt like I had been uprooted, like a potted plant that was dying and has been repotted in fresh soil and a bigger pot. I was building a new, more solid, deeper foundation within myself. You understand that Eagles and other bird species know when it's time to fly, but without ever having healthy examples in my life, I never felt I could fly. Now I had healthy examples and was beginning to soar, getting healthier every day. I learned to forgive and love the little boy inside. It was becoming okay to admit I didn't know how. That's a healthy way of speaking and feeling. Not trying to hide how dumb or stupid they made me feel was paramount and I nurtured that little boy and the man at the same time, becoming less and less shame-filled and releasing all that unbalanced energy. I learned to redirect those feelings to develop true and loving feelings for myself. I was nurturing my nature and I breathed easier, dropping my shoulders and releasing anxiety and stress. The self-hate, self-loathing, and self-doubt started to shift and fall away, creating new pathways for that little wounded boy who never knew how.

I was feeling and seeing the magic in my life as I began shapeshifting into various Spirit animals. Others started seeing the Spirit animals in me as well. One day, I was holding a healing session for my friend Audrey, who is a psychic medium. As I began, Audrey settled into the experience. But soon after I started, she began screaming in fear, scared out of her wits. I calmed her down and asked why she was screaming. She said I had shape shifted into a Grizzly Bear and held out her hands to show me how big my paws were. I was amazed at her telling me this. I assured her that it was safe and okay as it was part of my new-found medicine. I had no idea I had this ability, but quickly got comfortable with the idea and accepted it as normal. It felt natural to me. I knew things were happening in and around me but didn't realize it was to this extent.

At the end of that healing session, Audrey asked me, "Where is Shasta?" I asked why and she said, "You're supposed to go there, cleanse in the water with salt and let it fall on the rock." Mount Shasta, I reminded her, is up north and you know it. "No, I've never heard of it until now," she responded, "but you have to go there and cleanse." "Okay," I said, "I'll go there."

Another woman, Angela, friended me on FaceBook because of things I posted and said in my videos. She said she'd never heard a man talk like me before and at some point, would like to work with me. She even put a picture of her and I together as a potential promo photo. My wife Vanessa went through my computer and one day opened it to that picture and asked, "What is this?" in an accusatory way. You could have cut the tension with a knife. I told her exactly what it was, just a promo picture of Angela and I for potentially working together.

Oddly, being married I had never considered or thought of anything else. I found out later why she held an accusatory posture. She had begun working with a male mentor and I believe something was happening between them - otherwise, why would she speak to me in such an accusatory way? Besides, our marriage was ending or about to end and I didn't really care.

I decided to go to Mount Shasta. Angela lived in Ashland, Oregon, about an hour to an hour and a half north of Mount Shasta. We made plans to meet at the headwaters of the Sacramento River, the place where the river comes out of the rock. I had already made plans to stay with a family who I had done a long-distance emotional body reading for. They found me online and called me one day out of the blue, concerned about their daughter's emotional issues. I asked them to send me a photo of her and made a diagnosis. They were very happy to have an answer and invited me to spend two days in their home as their daughter wanted to meet me and make me breakfast.

It was a full moon. I left my home for Mount Shasta at midnight because I was so excited about what I was about to do. As I drove up Highway I-5, Grandmother moon was to my left riding my shoulder, accompanying me all the way through the San Joaquin Valley until the sun came up and I arrived somewhere in Sacramento. I stopped at an AM/PM gas station to sleep for an hour as I could barely keep my eyes open. I arrived at my host's home in Weed, California, just north of Shasta where I received shelter and fellowship for two days.

When I met with Angela, we sat on the grass and shared conversation. She brought gifts for me, a beautiful ceremonial cloth that had even more gifts wrapped inside. Protected in the cloth were two snakeskins from the shedding of serpents in her care and two Hawk feathers that she picked up along her journey. I was astonished and honored by these gifts. No one had ever given me anything like this and I could feel the power of this friendly offering. I had a rattle I made from Deer hooves, a Deer antler, and a smudge fan I made from Turkey feathers that I was gifted from an artist in Los Angeles. I was honored to give those elements as a gift as I felt so honored to be gifted in turn by Angela. We spent time down the river, sitting on the bank sharing stories and being eaten by ants and flies. We made our way back to the headwaters and did a ceremony standing in the water by smudging, drumming, and singing songs thanking Mother Earth for the water and each other. We made our way to Angela's car, hugging and thanking each other before she began her drive home to Ashland, Oregon.

I returned to the river with pink Himalayan salt I brought with me and did my cleansing ceremony, letting what was washed away fall on the rocks and make its way down the Sacramento River. Nothing changed right away, nor did I feel any different. I simply accepted that I had done what was asked of me and the rest would take care of itself.

I hosted a one-hour weekly online radio talk show called "Transformational Sacred Drum Medicine Show with Walking Crow," produced by Tiffany Michelle White Sage Woman of Goldylocks Productions in Groton, Connecticut. It was a weekly show where I was able to go deep into my intuitive self and do spiritual readings. Tiffany was very encouraging and one of my biggest fans. We became very good friends. She supported who I was, and it was obvious by the way she spoke to me. Sometimes I just talked about a particular chakra or chakras or had guests on to speak of their different modalities of healing and medicines. I brought on some of my teachers and interviewed them (which was the most fun). But mostly, the show helped me come into myself and my abilities in a strong and powerful way. The show eventually evolved into an online TV show which was even more fun with the ability to interface with guests and allowed viewers to put a face with the voice.

During the time I was married to Vanessa, I was also driving for Lyft and offering ride shares for extra cash. This afforded me the opportunity to sharpen my intuitive skills as well. I hung a small sign on the back panel of the passenger seat letting people know about my healing work. Some asked me to read them and I would turn around, look at them, and read their energy. After a while I was talking into the rearview mirror and not long after that I didn't even need to turn around to look at them. I was fully in my intuitive nature, reading their energy based on their voice and the little information they gave me. This, along with the radio show, really accelerated my abilities.

I don't know how I kept up with what was happening in my life or even whether I was keeping up at all. These experiences were becoming stories. I began speaking of how I was moving from point A to point B in my transformation and healing process. I shared these stories about how I was rooted and fruited on the radio show and at various events.

I felt I was coming into a different power. I would point to my sternum third chakra and say "Fire, Fuego. I can I will I do I am, I can I will I do I am, I can I will I do I am, I am the I am that I say I am." This became something I repeated to myself out loud, during healing sessions, at events, and during my live broadcasts. I believed every word and feeling of those words. I was empowering myself with the support of the spirit world and found no shame in my words. I was teaching this to my clients and others to help them move out of and overcome their low or no self-esteem. Wow! What a powerful tool of words and feeling, it changed the broken little boy. Who knew? Speaking of and to myself in this way could have been (and was) interpreted as conceit. One day, somebody told me, "You are pretty conceited, aren't you?" My response was, "You should have heard how I used to speak to myself."

In our house as kids and teenagers, we didn't praise or say kind things, we were always insulting and condescending and speaking down to each other. I never heard kind, encouraging, or supportive words from my parents, sisters, or brothers. So, at this late stage in life, I took the bull by the horns and began to transform my words into those of worthiness and self-esteem, giving myself permission to pull away from the pack. Even today within my family of origin, the same behavior exists and I make a great effort to hold my tongue with them, which isn't easy. I want to be me, not their perception of me. I don't want to separate myself, assume I may be better than them, or even appear that way. There is a price to pay for change and sometimes others won't or don't like it and will judge in a harsh way.

The phrase, "You always…" comes up often and stems from judgments. One day I made a statement and the, "You always…" phrase came up in an angry way. I responded, "I always…I always what? How old are you, still saying that?" I tried to ask it in a nice way, but there isn't really a nice way to let someone know they're immature, is there? Then again, those people are none of my business, are they?

Chapter 9: The Transcended Soul

One day, as I was working at the Los Angeles Sprouts Natural Food Store in the Vitamin department, I met a woman named Mina. I greeted her, saying hello, and she was open to conversation. She mentioned she lived in Sedona but was in town visiting her boyfriend for a few days. I had been to Sedona to do a fire ceremony, so I engaged in a "Sedonaesque" type conversation. I told her about my healing work and how I was interested in spending more time in Sedona learning more about the energy and spirit there. She shared the kind of work she did, where in Sedona she lived, and how she and her boyfriend wanted to start an intentional community there. We talked for a few minutes; she eventually said goodbye and left.

Mina later called and asked to meet. I didn't know it then, but she was apparently a life coach. We arranged to meet at a local eatery. We discussed her line of work and she continued to ask questions about what it is that I do, wondering if there was a way she could help me. I didn't know whether I needed a life coach but thanked her for thinking of me so highly. We said goodbye and went our separate ways.

Not long afterwards, I saw Mina again when she came into the store, this time with her boyfriend. She introduced us and we engaged in more conversation about Sedona as she inquired more about my work. She kindly invited me to come visit Sedona as she had an extra bedroom I could stay in. Her boyfriend seemed to be cool with it, so I said yes to the invitation. Again, Mina was a life coach so I thought it would be good to spend time around someone like her and maybe learn a little something from her.

While I was working at Sprouts, I was also house sitting, pet sitting, driving Lyft rideshare, working events, speaking at various engagements, making drums, and seeing clients. I slowly started trusting the universe. I knew I wouldn't get anywhere if I didn't trust. I began asking the universe for what I wanted and began making my way to escape and freedom. I began letting go of the jobs one at a time, first the pet sitting, then the house sitting. One day a customer at the store asked if we sold sage, I responded that we didn't, but I harvested sage and always carried it with me for just this sort of occasion. I explained that I didn't believe in purchasing sage and gave it as people needed and asked for it. I asked her to wait, went out to my car, opened the trunk, grabbed some sage, and closed the trunk when I stopped myself. I noticed the Lyft sticker on the rear window of my car, reopened the trunk, pulled it off, tossed it in the trash and went back inside the store to the waiting customer. I gave her the sage and asked her to use it in a good way. She graciously accepted, saying she would, and thanked me.

Removing the Lyft sticker was me taking another step closer to my goal. I eventually quit driving for Lyft rideshare.

I took Mina up on her invitation to visit Sedona and went for a few days. We hiked up Bell Rock, one of the most iconic vortexes in the Sedona area. I brought my 27-inch PowWow drum and a smaller drum with me. I had been doing online drum journeys, offering those who logged on to Facebook an opportunity to have the journey experience. Wearing headphones or earbuds, the drumming took them on a deep journey just by being still and allowing the sound and vibration to engulf their soul. The PowWow drum I used was made in Porterville, California, near the Eagle Mountain Reservation by a brother named Raymond Garcia.

Recommended by Sara Eagle Woman and her assistant, Raymond was native and had lived in the area all his life. I spent three days in Porterville with him and his family. Part of that journey was spent on the smooth Grandmother rocks and boulders, swimming in the Tule River and receiving the powerful energy from the sacred water. Over those three days, Raymond birthed a Cowhide Drum for me. I assisted in cutting ties from the giant hide to be used making the drum. On the third day, she was complete and the only thing left was to let her dry. I packed her in my car and made my way back to Los Angeles.

Drumming in Sedona was a dream come true. One late afternoon, Mina and I made our way to Bell Rock with PowWow drum in tow to present a live drum journey broadcast on Facebook. Darkness fell early, though, and I was kind of bummed because I wanted to drum on Bell Rock. As it was already dark, we stopped where we were to set the drum up for the journey. I put up a tripod with a camera but there was no way for the viewers to see because it was so dark. But actually, who needed their eyes for this kind of journey? We began the live broadcast and as I started drumming, a strong breeze came from the saddle between Bell Rock and Courthouse Butte. When I felt the breeze, I knew exactly what it was and started smiling as I understand what was happening. I drummed for twenty-five minutes, enjoying the presence of the spirits and ancient ones that were with me. Mina also noticed and mentioned what was happening as the breeze came up. The journey ended as I slowed the drumming to call all the souls journeying with us back to their bodies.

After the journey, Mina asked if we could just lay in the dark and look up at the stars. I don't remember how long we laid there, but we eventually picked up our things and made our way back to her house, about five blocks away. I slept like a baby that night, feeling good and proud of myself for taking the time to honor the spirits in the process. It is said that the spirits love it when we sing and drum, but they really love it when we dance. So, every time I sing and drum or just drum for the journey, I make sure to move my feet and dance. A'ho!

The next day when I woke up, I spent quiet time at Mina's in the bedroom I was occupying. I was just staring out the window when my phone rang. It was Dana Maginnis. She asked how I was doing and we made the usual small talk. She asked if I had done ceremony the night before and in a nonchalant way I said no, I just drummed at Bell Rock for a journey. She stopped me and said, "Anthony! You know that ceremony was for you." I giggled saying, "Yes, you're right. Why?"

Dana told me that she had a dream about me drumming at night in a canyon. I was surrounded by ancient elders and in between them were giant Crow feathers. I was amazed at what she was telling me, and it made the breeze I experienced last night make more sense. Wow! This was powerful. Not only our separate experiences, but how we are connected to each other and the spirit world.

Aspects of my language began to change as well. At first, I was somewhat embarrassed about using the spirit or star language, but Grandmother Chee, a Navajo/Diné native, told me to speak it or sing it without question and always say yes. My words changed as well, as I spoke to and for my higher and better good (God). The guides and spirits were giving me alternate words and ways of speaking, which improved my self-esteem. Over the years, I taught others to do the same. I would stop them mid-sentence and ask them to use a word that the guides and spirits wanted them (and myself) to use. I always tried to do this as gently as possible, as we humans have fragile egos.

The spirit world was downloading, and I was channeling songs in the spirit or star language. I was using their words in ceremonies for the public and myself to heal. In public, I sang only in the spirit language. But when I was alone, singing and drumming on the land or at home, Spirit would reveal the meaning of the songs, helping me transform my emotional body. They would have me sing the words in a particular order and I still do that to this day. I would sing them on my radio show or on live Facebook broadcasts. The general public started responding positively and it came to light that people were singing these songs on hikes, ceremonies, or while just walking through a forest. People were healing their own emotional bodies through the songs even without knowing the meanings.

I was making lots of drums and as I progressed, the guides and spirits showed me new ways to tie, braid, or weave the ties in different ways and designs. They weren't elaborate, but each began to take on its own personality. I eventually made a 20" inch Bear drum for myself and carry that powerful medicine to this day. I used a lot of available plant medicine to create the sacred water for birthing the drum medicine I was manifesting. I traveled from Los Angeles to Sedona more often, staying with my new friend Mina. I began to visit shop owners to introduce myself, my mode of healing, and my drums.

I introduced myself to a woman I was told I needed to see. Phaedra was native and had recently opened a studio called Tribe Wellness. She had a comfortable demeanor. We took a liking to each other and arranged for me to teach and hold events at the studio. When I went to the studio for my first event, I walked in and Phaedra asked, "Why do I feel Colombian energy off of you?" I laughed and responded, "This medicine bag I carry was purchased in the Candelaria Barrio of Bogota, Columbia long before I stepped into my work." I placed it on the table in front of her and took out my rattle saying, "This is also from Colombia." We both understood and started laughing. This kind of thing happened more and more often around the intuitives I spent time with.

One occasion when I visited my mom's home in Los Angeles, I experienced anxiety. The televisions were always on loud with CNN or some kind of thing over and over. I couldn't stand it as I don't watch TV or news that isn't really news at all. I hadn't fully completed the work with my mother, but I was itching to get the heck out of there.

When I was preparing to leave, I told mom, "I gotta get out of here, I'm going back to Sedona." Crying, Mom said, "I don't want you to leave." I ignored her plea and left the next morning at 4:00am, heading for Sedona in a torrential downpour. Now you must know, I never ever left my mom for any length of time without having her give me a blessing. I just didn't do that. But this time, I told her I was leaving at 4:00am and didn't want to wake her up.

When 4:00am came, I quietly loaded what was left of my luggage, pointed my car east, and drove off. It was an uneasy beginning to my travels because I knew my mom was upset about me leaving and to make matters worse, I went against my better judgment and bypassed her beautiful blessing. It was pouring cats and dogs; I mean sideways rain and flooded freeways. I drove under the speed limit in the center lane. Westbound traffic was backed up for miles and all I could see was a river of headlights. Every now and again the lights and sounds of emergency vehicle sirens pierced the darkness. There was almost no traffic moving in my direction, but I stayed in the middle lane under the speed limit because of hydroplaning.

I was in San Bernardino when I saw a faint light flash at me and a man with glasses standing on the freeway in the rain. I turned to see him and when I turned my eyes back to the road, I saw the silhouette of a car through the darkness with no lights on stalled in the lane in front of me. I swerved to miss the car but clipped it with my right rear fender and went into a spin. I don't remember how many times my car spun but when it stopped, I felt like I was out of my body. I got out and the rear right wheel had been torn completely off.

Cars began hitting the stranded car and as I tried to stay out of the way, an eighteen-wheeler came barreling down the highway breaking cautiously trying to avoid the mayhem. I had to run out of the way to avoid being hit. A Highway Patrolman appeared and directed people to move their cars to the side of the road. I got back in my car and was able to drive it and myself out of harm's way. What was I going to do and who was I going to call? I sat in my car soaking wet when an ambulance paramedic came over to check on me, asking whether I needed medical assistance or needed to go to the hospital. I was disoriented. At first, I said yes and started making my way to the ambulance, but then I stopped myself and said, "No, I don't need to go to the hospital."

Just then a flatbed tow truck showed up and the driver asked if I needed a tow. I said yes without knowing where I would have it towed to. I asked if there was a parking lot nearby that he could tow me to, thinking it was best to get off the freeway because of my luggage, ceremonial tools, and drums. He said there was a Stater Brothers Market nearby, but it was going to cost me $240.00. My AAA membership had expired, so I had no choice but to say, "Yes, let's do it." My car was loaded up and we pulled off the freeway into a parking lot where he unloaded it. I sat in my car still wet and in shock from the accident, just wanting to be warm and dry. I let my car run just to stay warm. What should I do? Just then, Spirit told me to send an SOS out on social media to see if someone in the area could help.

I received a response from Theresa Smith, a Chiropractor and friend with an office in Monrovia where I rented healing space. She said she would come and get me and would be there as soon as possible. While I was waiting, I went across the street to a fast-food restaurant to use the bathroom (I'd had a lot of coffee). On the way out, I was walking through the parking lot when out of the corner of my eye I saw a red car coming out of the drive thru, heading straight for me. I yelled and jumped in the air, but the car hit me anyway.

Oh my gosh, did this just happen? I landed on the hood of the car. The lady freaked out and was terrified. I don't know if she was as terrified as I was after my already frightening experience on the freeway. I rolled off the hood and went around the driver's side, yelling at her through the window, "What's the matter with you?" She seemed to be as scared as I was and kept apologizing and asking if she should call an ambulance. I felt no breaks or anything else physically wrong, but we exchanged information, and I went back to my car.

It only seemed like minutes after I was back in my warm car when glancing left, to my surprise there was Theresa. She parked next to me, coming to the rescue just like magic. I believe it was. We transferred everything that was in my car to hers and she drove me back to her office to change out of my wet clothes. Afterwards, she asked me to get on her examining table and began to adjust me, bringing me back into my body. I realized as the accident was happening and the car was spinning, I could feel myself becoming splintered. I let Theresa do her work and relaxed through the process.

When my car spun out of control, I felt my upper body vibrating back and forth from side to side, almost like a character in the cartoons I used to watch as a child. Having Theresa's healing hands and energy work on me so early in the game was good for me. After our session, we got back into Theresa's car and she drove me all the way to my mother's home in the San Fernando Valley. The distance between my mom's and the place in San Bernardino where the accidents happened is not close. It was quite a drive, but my dear friend did not have a problem with taking care of me and tucking me under her wing. There are people who will call you friend but treat you like a complete stranger most of the time. Not Theresa, she went above and beyond. I can never repay her for what she did for me that morning. She never asked me for a dime or showed resentment as sometimes happens with people when they do a kind act. I'm not judging other people, but I am He Who Notices, and I definitely know who in my life I could call on.

When we arrived at mom's, I unloaded my things from Theresa's car into her garage and profusely thanked Theresa for her help and being a wonderful human being. I invited her in to meet mom, but she declined and drove off. I took a deep breath before I walked in the house as I knew there was a lot to explain about why I was back. As I opened the door and went inside, mom looked over her shoulder to see who was coming in, as it was strange for somebody to enter her house without knocking first. With a surprised look she asked, "What are you doing here?" I took a deep breath and began telling her about my strange morning odysseys. She was clearly upset, but didn't say a lot, she was just glad I wasn't hurt.

But was I hurt? It wasn't outwardly visible, but I was not okay and didn't know how to be okay after those traumatic ordeals. I expressed to mom that I never should have left the way I did and that I was sorry for leaving. I really wanted to be in Sedona and inside I kept telling myself I needed to be there instead of at my mom's. It would be weeks before I could return to Sedona. I no longer had a permanent home in Los Angeles, so I stayed with mom until Spirit said it was okay for me to go.

Days after the accident, my friend and healer Dana Maginnis called to see if I was okay. She could feel my trauma from the accidents and wanted to help, so I went to her office for a healing session. I was apparently still not fully aligned after the accidents, so I got on Dana's table and she went to work. At the beginning, I could see a round stained glass spinning slowly down towards me. I felt Saint Germain energy descending upon my body. I could also see Blue Kachina, also known as Blue Star Kachina or Saquasohuh. Blue Star Kachina is a Hopi Kachina or spirit that signifies the coming of the beginning of the new world by appearing in the form of a Blue Star. And here it was, looking in on me while Dana worked. Also with me was a native spirit wearing buckskin with braided hair, two feathers on the top of his head, and his arms crossed in front of him. He didn't look straight at me that I recall, he just looked off into the distance. I believe his name was Two Feathers and I found comfort knowing he and the others were with me. Over the weeks, Dana continued working on me and the three were present in my awareness during each session. I always knew when the session was coming to an end as the stained glass and Saint Germain energy reversed their spin to rise back up to the heavens.

Throughout the years, I had made friends across the country and around the world. They were healers, readers, mystics, psychic mediums, witches, native peoples, shamans, and massage therapists of all types. My circles were growing. I made friends with Shaman Isabella Stoloff from Fullerton, California. For some reason I reached out to her after my accident. We were familiar with each other's names through our reputations and individual work. We spoke for a while and part of our conversation was about the accidents. I had to ask myself, "Were those really accidents?"

She invited me to her house for a Full Moon Fire Ceremony. I borrowed my mom's car even though I was pretty fucked up emotionally and physically from the accidents. Walking around, I could feel the numbness in my soul. I was really a wreck. I went to the ceremony even though I was not 100% sure about driving. It was raining that night which really made me uneasy, but I did it anyway. I drove carefully and safely and arrived for the ceremony. Isabella greeted me at the door, and I felt welcomed and at home in her small warm house.

She had asked me to bring one of the drum mallets I made, because she needed a new one. I was happy to gift it to her. I met a lot of very nice people that night who were happy to meet me. Eventually we moved out to the yard to hold ceremony, which was incredible. The clouds opened and we could see the moon in her fullness against a dark sky filled with stars and lingering clouds. After ceremony we went back into the house and shared a feast together. The kind folks had brought all kinds of delicious food to share. After eating and fellowship, I thanked Isabella and everyone, then made my way gingerly back to the San Fernando Valley forty miles to the north.

After some time, I rented a car and drove to Sedona for a weekend. I felt so much better. I wasn't desperate to be there and Sedona wasn't desperate to have me, lol. I went to pick up some things I'd left behind at my friend Roberto's and stayed with him for three days. While I was there, Phaedra called and asked if I was in town. I said yes, for a couple of days, and asked why. She said there was a party at the studio and wanted me to come. I told her I would be there and hung up. Then I thought, "What's the party for?" I called her back and asked, she said it was a birthday party for her mom, Rima Thundercloud.

I was taught never to show up empty handed, so I made my way to the store to purchase flowers and a card for the birthday girl even though we had ever met. I arrived at Tribe Wellness and the party was jumping. I said hello to Phaedra and others and asked Phaedra where I could find her mom. She pointed me in her direction. I walked over, introduced myself, wished her a Happy Birthday, and presented her with the card and flowers.

I served myself some food and found a place across the room from Rima Thundercloud. While I was eating, she came over, sat next to me, and started making small talk. Now, Phaedra, her daughter, is a known intuitive and psychic and I would even say a medicine woman. I could tell Rima knew her stuff and was a medicine woman and an artist herself. She sat next to me for a reason, and I knew something was coming. As she made small talk, I waited and sure enough it came forth. She said, "I'm just gonna spit it out." And I responded, "I wish you would!"

Rima began, "I see you're surrounded by feathers. There is a headdress on the floor, when are you going to pick it up?" I knew the jig was up. I had been avoiding my real work and dragging my feet to my true and deeper self. I knew exactly what she meant and why she was saying it. It was time to step up for myself because nobody else could do it for me.

A couple of days later, I was back in Los Angeles making drums, seeing clients, and attending sweat lodge. Being in Los Angeles allowed me the opportunity to heal the relationship with mom. Not on her part, strictly on mine. I had lots of work to do towards that but didn't know where to start.

In May of 2019, I got a palsy in my eye and had to wear a patch to allow me to see straight and drive. I also experienced what I believed was neuropathy in two thirds of my body. I had chronic pain and wasn't sure how to heal it. I felt extremely weak with no appetite and some days couldn't even get out of bed. I went to the doctor and asked them to check me for Lyme disease because I spent so much time out in the canyons and mountains. I couldn't say I was bitten by a tick, but there was always that outside chance as I would drum sitting in the dirt, tall grass or chaparral amongst the trees and forest.

I traveled back and forth between Sedona and New River, staying with my friend Wendy and her family. While I was there, my friend Cheryl Crain Gentry offered a Myofascial healing. It hurt like heck because of the chronic pain. She also felt I might have Lyme disease. She tried to be as gentle as possible, but I was in so much pain I don't know how I allowed that healing. Later, Cheryl and a group of what I call Grandmothers made drums with me in Cave Creek. It was an honor to make drums with this beautiful group.

I spent some time staying with Wendy, Grace, and Jerry in their New River home, more like a small farm or ranch. Staying with them was comfortable for me, they were a small family with dogs and chickens. Wendy and I would sit outside in the mornings, with me drumming and singing as we sipped our coffee. When I stayed with them previously, I birthed sacred drums on the property. This was an honor for me, as I didn't feel called to do this everywhere. I birthed three drums as Wendy watched. She asked if she could birth the last drum of the four. I agreed and she assembled the Buffalo hide drum. As she worked, I told her the drum she was birthing was going to be hers. She was excited and asked if she could tie a stone or crystal onto the drum as a handle. How could I say no to that? It was going to be hers and I wanted the drum to be the way she wanted it, fully hers. It was a great pleasure to watch her work her own medicine into her medicine drum.

Another time, we held a Full Moon Ceremony there and Wendy invited neighbors and friends to attend. We had a group of about twenty or so and none of them had ever sat in this kind of ceremony or had even met me until now. I didn't realize it, but we were all about to experience some of the things that had already been happening in my medicine as I said YES. I prepared the area by smudging and opened the portal to the spirit world by smoking the pipe, offering tobacco. I created a fire as the center of the sacred circle. During the ceremony, I smudged all participants, and they had the opportunity to take tobacco, create intentions of what they wanted to let go of emotionally, and infuse those things into the tobacco by holding it to their heart before offering it to the fire. I drummed and sang medicine songs as the group meditated on their intentions.

During the ceremony, I could see the Full Moon rising in the east from my vantage point. As it rose, I invited the group to turn and watch her rise. What an experience. As the group sat quietly watching Grandmother Moon rise, a Great Horned Owl flew across the moon from south to north. They all gasped in wonder asking how I did it and if it was some sort of trick. It was an amazing, auspicious thing to have them experience this on their first Full Moon Fire Ceremony with me. I couldn't have planned it that way if I wanted to, but spirit and animal spirits were with me. Why wouldn't they be? These kinds of things happened more and more once I said YES to the journey, in different ways and experiences.

Early on in my journey, I was driving Lyft rideshare when I picked up a client in the city of Pasadena. The gentleman was of Indian origin and worked in technology in the area. I headed towards his destination in an unfamiliar part of the city and as I exited the freeway, I noticed a heavy amount of traffic. We were in a shopping mall area, but it was strange that we were experiencing heavy traffic considering the time of day. Coming to a red light, for some reason I accelerated through it with traffic moving in every direction.

I froze and looked at my passenger in the rearview mirror. His eyes were bugging out of the sockets due to surprise and fear. As we made our way through the intersection, I realized we were not getting hit or hitting other cars. I also noticed we were not on the ground, we seemed to be carried above the traffic then placed down gently on the other side of the intersection without harm. Wow! It was an incredible experience that had never happened before. Or maybe it had and I just never noticed because of my closed mind. I apologized to my passenger and said, "I never go through red lights." And, laughing a bit, followed up with, "I can't say that anymore." My life certainly was changing. There were other experiences like this to share, but who could believe me?

Chapter 10: The Guide Within

One day, I received a call from a lady living in Sedona. She asked if I did land clearings, explaining that she had an entity on her property and wondered if I could help clear it. I told her I could, so we scheduled a time for me come to Sedona and meet her in her home. We arranged for me to stay the night in a downstairs room, separate from the main house. At the same time, I had a friend in Cottonwood who was opening a new business. She had asked me for sage bundles for her grand opening as she knew I harvested and tied my own. I went to the grand opening, delivered the sage bundles, spent time with her guests to support her new business, had a bite of food, and left for the Village of Oak Creek in Sedona to do the clearing of the home.

After arriving in Oak Creek, I stopped in a local convenience market to buy a bottle of water and some snacks. As I walked in the door, I heard a voice call out, "Hey, Walking Crow!" This was the first time I heard someone call me by my name in that way. The man who called out worked at the store and apparently followed me on social media. I was on quite a few social media bulletin boards and slowly receiving recognition and developing a following for the work I was doing. This made me feel good about how far I had come in such a short time. People in Sedona were becoming aware of who I was and that felt encouraging.

From there, I drove four blocks to the home where the clearing was needed. It was just below a beautiful Red Rock formation called Castle Rock. I didn't know it then, but one day I would find myself climbing Castle Rock to do ceremony on a high shelf that jetted out (called the diving board), overlooking the Village of Oak Creek. I arrived at my destination and was welcomed by the owners of the property.

When I walked in, the husband was building a fire ring in the living room and the wife was texting and calling back and forth with someone. I could feel lots of frantic and stressful energy in the house that had nothing to do with an entity, only with the belief of an entity. I asked why her husband was building a fire ring in the house and the wife responded, "I'm on the phone with a white witch from Switzerland and she is looking into the house remotely. That means she has the ability to see everything in the house without being in it or ever having been in it. She wants us to build a fire for a clearing ceremony and me to hold a crystal in my hand." I could feel her husband's stress and embarrassment about building the fire ring in the middle of the living room. I asked, "Did you say she was viewing remotely?" The wife answered yes, and I then asked, "If she can see your house remotely, why can't she see the fireplace in the living room?"

A man will do just about anything for his wife to keep her happy. I know I did for my first wife when I moved across the country to Tennessee. But really, how far should a man go for the neurotic woman he loves? I could tell he was embarrassed in front of a man he had never met before. The only thing I said to him was, "It's okay, you don't have to do that."

I could feel the husband's relief without saying a word. He stopped what he was doing as I said to his wife, "We can use your fireplace, you don't want to burn your house down." I couldn't help but laugh inside. She then took me into a bedroom and showed me a ceiling fan where the white witch told her the entity came through. Again, I couldn't help it, but didn't let her see me roll my eyes. I know some people want to believe anything, but this was ridiculous.

I asked her if I could walk through the house and over the entire property and she said yes. Meanwhile, she was still texting and calling and back and forth with the white witch. After walking the property, I reentered the house and asked the wife to hang up the phone and stop texting. I also asked her why she had asked me to come if she was already working with someone. I told her, "You are either going to work with her or me, but either way you're going to pay me. You must understand, sometimes people with issues other than entities don't know they have issues." Oh boy! Some will believe that more is better but that's not necessarily true, it simply makes things more confusing. She was making herself stressed and anxiety-filled over something that didn't have to be so difficult.

I asked the husband to bring in firewood so I could properly build a fire in the fireplace. I asked her to bring me bowls and tea candles, one for each room of the house including the garage and downstairs area. I placed the bowls with water in each room, floating a tea candle in each one. Before I did this, I smudged myself with sage to clear myself of any of the energies in the house. You may not believe so, but stress

page 89

and anxiety are low vibrational energies brought on by fear. Fear of what? Good question. Humans have been conditioned through many sources to be afraid of their own shadows. There's always a boogie man lurking around every corner and in every thought. Just listen closely to the way people talk to themselves and others, thinking something is gonna happen so they are guarded and riddled with fear. Their fear has a kung fu grip over them. I believe this is why people consume alcohol, drugs of every kind, tobacco, food, and worst of all television.

After smudging and clearing myself, I smoked my pipe with tobacco to open the portal to the spirit world. I lit the fire in the fireplace, placed sage and tobacco on the fire, and began singing a medicine song. After drumming, singing, and thanking Great Spirit for being present, I asked the wife and husband to allow me to smudge them. Again, I realized the husband was going along with his wife just to appease her.

I walked through the house, smudging every room, closet, and cubby hole in it. Going out to the yard, I walked the property and smudged the yard paying very close attention to my surroundings. Reentering the house, I again smoked the pipe and blew smoke into every room, opening the portals in each space. I then went from room to room lighting the tea candles in the bowls we had placed in each room. I took my rattle and began to go from room to room again, rattling and telling the lower energies or entities they were not welcome in the house. I repeated this over and over again in each and every space. I must admit, I didn't believe one word of the story about an entity coming through the fan and chuckled about it as I rattled my way around.

The tea candles took some time to burn through. When they extinguished, one by one I picked up the bowls and dumped the water into the toilet, flushing it and closing the lid (to close the door on it if you will). I did this with each bowl of water, then took the lady of the house out into the yard and told her, "This is ancient land and there are still ancient spirits living on this land."

I took her to the edge of the yard and showed her a small space along the edge of the property. I asked her to create a space about two feet by two feet or four by four, surrounded by rocks with an opening for the spirits to go in and out. A space where no one else would enter but them. It would be their home and give them a sense of belonging. This would keep them out of the house.

I was surprised at her response when she said, "This is my house and I'm not going to do that." Hearing her say that I wondered what this was all about. Was it just the drama of it all and her having a sense of relief about believing it was an entity? I was bewildered. I explained, "Not the house, the land the house is on and the surrounding area. These spirits don't know where to go as they have no home."

I was invited to stay in their home for a few days and after a few days, was invited to stay for two months. I eventually rented the room for an additional month while I was in Sedona as I had no home of my own yet.

During that time, I met a woman named Kelly who found me vending my drums at a local art fair in the Village of Oak Creek. As we talked, she started crying and asked me why I was talking to her about Alcoholics Anonymous. I responded that I wasn't talking about Alcoholics Anonymous, she was. I shared that I had been sober for over twenty-five years, which surprised her. I then asked if I could read her energy. A wave of extreme sadness came over her and she couldn't stop crying. I read her emotional body and asked if I could place my hand on her back over the place of her heart and she said yes. I placed my hand on her back over her heart space, allowing her to receive warm healing energy. When she was done receiving, Kelly moved forward, tried a few different drums, and chose a fifteen-inch Elk hide drum. We did an exchange ceremony which I offer to all the individuals that purchase my drums.

As time went on, Kelly and I began to see each other romantically. It was nice as we both loved the land and enjoyed spending time on it together. We often hiked, stopping to offer tobacco to Mother Earth, drumming, and singing medicine songs. Our time together was comfortable. Often, we would get together at her house to watch movies on cold winter nights. I didn't know it until later, but she was friends with the lady who owned the house where I did the clearing. Kelly would come over to see me or go out to dinner and when she visited the lady of the house, she'd pop downstairs to see me for a bit.

One day Kelly received the news that she was going to have to put her dog Brandy down. This broke her heart, and I couldn't help but feel her pain as her little one was the sweetest dog. Brandy was older and getting close to that time. It was especially hard for Kelly because she had traveled extensively throughout the United States with Brandy accompanying her everywhere. They were inseparable. Kelly made arrangements with the veterinarian and set a date. She let her adult children and her ex-husband know about Brandy, then asked if I would do a crossing over ceremony for her. I had never met Kelly's children or ex-husband, but Kelly had told them about me and they were glad I was there supporting her through this time. Kelly's children lived in different parts of the country and her ex-husband in New Jersey.

The day arrived. The veterinarian came to Kelly's and prepared for what was about to happen. How do you prepare for such a thing? You can't really, you just have to experience it and go through the process. It is difficult making such a decision for the good of the animal. I mean, why should anyone or anything suffer?

We video-conferenced with Kelly's children and ex-husband. I smudged myself, the veterinarian, the little one, and Kelly along with the computers where her family was in video conference with us, clearing unwanted energies. I lit the pipe and covered myself in smoke to open the portal to the spirit world. I blew tobacco smoke over Brandy and began to rattle for a bit to clear the static energy and bring all involved into their hearts. I then sang several medicine songs and thanked the spirit world for the soul of this little Brandy and her place in all our lives.

Kelly held Brandy as the veterinarian injected her in the leg and she slowly went to sleep. She crossed over into the North in the medicine wheel, the place of our ancestors, winter, wisdom, and the place of rest when we cross over. The veterinarian then took Brandy in her arms and went out the door. Brandy was going to be cremated and the ashes returned to Kelly in a couple of weeks. I held space for Kelly and the family, staying out of the way honoring their need to grieve.

When the ashes were delivered weeks later, Kelly and I set out to release some on the land at Bell Rock, one of her favorite places. We did this several times as it helped Kelly with her grieving. Late in October, the place I was renting for a month told me they needed the space back, so I began looking for another place to live. Kelly was going to be leaving for New Jersey during the Holidays beginning in November, so I asked if I could stay at her house and pay the bills while she was gone. Kelly said yes, which was great by me. I was at Kelly's after she left and made drums in the garage. It was cold, so I would make the drums with the garage door open and a space heater always blowing on me. I wanted to look out at nature as I made drums and was willing to bear the cold.

Kelly returned in February and when she returned, something had changed. She was standoffish. I did not want to be there when she returned, as she had been gone for some time and I wanted to allow her time to be home on her own. I had already secured a place in the town of Cornville not far away, so we said our goodbyes and I left.

I moved into and shared a home with a local Sedona artist named Clark. It was a beautiful place, where I could not only live, but have an office and could see clients for healing, with space for making drums and rattles. I did a lot of live videos from my office and even held private drum birthing ceremonies with clients there.

Interesting that all I had to do to be and live in Sedona was to let go of the wanting and the desperation of trying to be here instead of Los Angeles. I not only had to change my feeling and thinking about it, but I also had to change my language. I had to learn to be at peace with my surroundings wherever I was. The more I surrendered to myself, the better I felt, and the better things got. This is a concept I learned in AA but obviously hadn't fully integrating in my life until now. Even my language about mom changed when I stopped fighting myself and telling myself I had to leave. I didn't realize how much it was hurting both her and me. My thoughts and words were pulling us apart when all I wanted was to be at peace with her.

Chapter 11: The Embodiment

After two or three years of moving back and forth between Sedona and Los Angeles, I settled down and eventually found a great home in Sedona owned by my friend Kathy. She had purchased it for her mom, Mary, to live out her final years. At the time, I was staying in Kathy's home just a few blocks away; she offered it to me until I found a place of my own. When Mary passed, I supported Kathy through her time of grief. A few weeks had gone by when I asked her what she was going to do with her mom's place. It was the bottom unit of a triplex she had purchased for her mom a few years earlier. It was in a beautiful area of the Village of Oak Creek, on a golf course surrounded by the mountains of Bell Rock, Court House Butte, Castle Rock, and Wild Horse Mesa.

It would be a perfect place to live, see clients, make drums, and rattles, and practice my medicine. Kathy asked if I wanted to rent it and I said YES. She asked whether I could afford it and I replied YES. Shortly after that, I called a client also named Anthony that I had seen earlier that year and asked if he still wanted to move to Sedona. He said YES and I asked him to send the deposit and first month's rent. I not only had a new home, but a roommate as well. That is how things work out when we say YES to ourselves.

I held ceremony before moving in, taking my sage, drums, rattles, and medicine bag over to the apartment to clear energies. Kathy's mom's energy was still in the home and I wanted to be respectful of them both. I knew Mary would eventually move to the spirit world, so I didn't push her or speak to her strongly about leaving. I caught glimpses of her from time to time and could even smell her perfume.

She liked to watch me from around corners while I was working or moving through the house. I believe she thought I couldn't see her; she was too cute for a spirit. This made me giggle and I would let her know I could see her. She hung around long enough to know Kathy would be all right, while Kathy moved through the emotions and paperwork of letting go. I am glad I supported and was there for her, she gave her mother so much and in truth in our short time as friends, she gave me a lot with love and support. Meeting Kathy earlier at a Star Knowledge Peace Conference in Blythe, California has been an amazing part of my being in Sedona. She became part of the foundation of Tribe I was building in my new surroundings.

Kathy later purchased a house on the Dolores River in Colorado and invited me to stay for weeks at a time as we put her new home in order. We cleaned cupboards, closets, went on adventures in nature, and spent hours on the river's banks, drumming and singing medicine songs. Kathy opened her arms to me as a brother and a friend and gave me a place to escape or rest from my life in Sedona. Dolores is a small town of about a thousand residents with a park and a great local gourmet market which we loved. They have a farmer's market at the park for anybody who grows vegetables or baked goods, with frybread, arts and crafts. It is the way I always imagined community. Everybody knew who you were, and I was willing to extend a hand and become a part of the community even though I didn't live there full time. I even made a point to introduce myself to one of the county Sheriff Deputies named Issac, who just happened to be Navajo. For a town with a thousand residents, Dolores had a big spiritual and artist community. We fit right in.

As my work expanded in Sedona and I continued building my foundation, I spent less and less time in Dolores with Kathy. This wasn't on purpose; it was just the way the flow had us moving. Kathy still owns a house in Sedona just blocks from me and we spend time together when she's in town. Kathy always invites me to Dolores, and I hope to return as soon as possible as I carry that land and its people in my heart. I miss the solitude and beauty of the river and the way spirit and nature speaks to me when I'm there.

On any given day, you can find me birthing drums at sunrise after ceremonially placing the animal hide medicine in the sacred waters at sunset the night before. For me this is symbolic of creation or procreation/co-creation as Grandfather Sun sets in the ocean waters of the west seeking his lover Grandmother Moon. I was never taught how to birth drums, so the symbolic nature of how I've been guided to do this by the spirits is important to me. I never waiver from my methodology or my tradition in this lifetime of birthing medicine drums.

Teaching and inviting others to do this with me is a powerful experience. Participants are with me for about six hours over a two-day period to ceremonially birth their own medicine drums, sitting with the elements of tree/frame (Grandmother) and the animal hide of their choice. Prior to this, they experience creating the sacred water or womb using tobaccos and plant medicines local to Sedona. Everything that goes into the sacred water (womb) comes from the earth. Cacao is also placed in the water as part of my lineage of Mexico and Mixica connection along with sacred dirt from El Santuario de Chimayó in New Mexico. It is said the dirt from this small church has healing properties and if you go there, you will see the pictures of all who have been healed by the magic of this tiny church. When I go to Chimayó to collect dirt, I first smudge when I enter and make an offering of my sacred tobacco to the church and the land. There is a pit where one can collect the sacred dirt. I take only what will be needed until the next time I travel to New Mexico.

The sacred water softens the hide during the night, after a short ceremony placing the animal into the sacred water of the womb while Grandfather Sun goes to sleep in the west and chases his beloved Grandmother Moon. At sunrise the next morning, I say hello to the sun and thank Great Spirit, Great Mother, the power and guidance of the Medicine Wheel, and all our Relations. I start my morning ritual of smudging the new morning, myself, my tools, the table holding the sacred womb with the water, sacred medicines and hides in it. I then smoke the pipe to open the portal between myself, the elements, the sacred animal that gifted the hide, and grandmother (the frame), along with the tools and table. Then and only then do I begin the process of birthing the drum medicine. I will birth anywhere from one to four drums beginning at sunrise and will always be finished with the process no later than ten or eleven that morning. Then it's a matter of tending to the drums, checking on them to make sure they are drying properly, doting over them one by one until they are fully dry and ready to be played. The drying process can take up to three days depending on the weather at the time.

As I became rooted in Sedona, I began to embody not just what I was doing, but how I spoke of it. I call it "Transformational Sacred Drum Medicine" and as I moved deeper into my work, I began to embody exactly what that meant. I am Transformational, I am Sacred, I am the Drum, I am Medicine. I embodied this by doing and speaking the truth of what I had become. I didn't wait for permission from society or community; I evolved by listening and doing what was asked of me by the spirit world. There was nobody patting me on the back or supporting me financially. I simply took my life, body, and soul into my own hands and moved forward by saying YES to myself. I stopped living with self-doubt. I empowered myself with my YES, my doing, and my being. There were no rules, certificates, right or wrong ways, there was only YES, doing and being.

What will you say yes to after a lifetime of no? I ask my clients and audiences this question to get their attention, because as humans we say no to ourselves more than we realize. Much of our life is missed because we are busy living someone else's life or trying to live up to someone else's idea of what or who we should be. I know, because I missed a lot in my life because of "Do this, do that, don't do this and don't do that." I tried to be what others wanted me to be. I watched TV and tried to keep up with the Joneses. Fuck the Joneses! I have my life to live and I am living my best life. I'm not a joiner, I'm a 'be'er.' After a lifetime of not having one, I will always follow my path. I won't let anyone change my mind because I follow my heart, and only I know my heart.

What do you know, what do you do, do you do *you* or are you tethered to the pole? People pleasing is not an attractive trait, it is ugly and allows your low or lack of self-esteem to be fully present. Learn to live in your fullness, not as a fool chasing compliments, or love, or simply trying to be liked. Stand on your own by honoring what the universe gave you to run the race. You are the most important person in your world. Not your partner, children, brothers, sisters, parents, society, or community can give you permission to be the true you. Alcoholics Anonymous says you can't give away what you haven't got. When you get on a jet plane, they ask you to put the mask on yourself *first*.

What are you waiting for? Why wouldn't you say YES to yourself? No one will love you like only you can love you, so stop waiting to be saved. The time is here and now and there is no savior. You are your savior and your best and only love…

Like Bob Marley said, *"Get Up, Stand Up."*

A'ho Mitakuiasi! All my Relations! ~ Walking Crow,
Transformational Sacred Drum Medicine

Conclusion

Some years back, I was sitting one day at my mother's dining room table while she was clipping coupons. I was talking about how when I was a young boy, I would sit in our Plum tree at the house in the old neighborhood where we used to live. I would sit in that tree for hours during summer in the cool shade of the canopy the branches created, by myself, eating the juicy plums one after another. Mom was preoccupied and wasn't listening, or should I say only half listening. I was recounting this story and the still small voice inside asked me to stop talking and look up the meaning of Plum tree. I pulled out my phone and Googled "Plum tree." When I read the meaning, I was deeply touched and surprised. In Asia and the Far East, the Plum Tree is the "Tree of Life." Wow, was I surprised!

I had been sitting in that beautiful "Tree of Life," and partaking of its life-giving fruit for years. I speak often of how trees are Grandmothers that see all things, the sun, the moon, the stars, the other trees, the animals, the birds in the sky, the rain plants and all of us. But Grandmother trees never see themselves. They give their fruit, their wood, they lay down their lives daily, and here I was as a young boy, being held by a grandmother I didn't know until I grew into manhood. She held me in her branches, cradling my sweet, lonely soul, feeding me from the fruit of her bounty and breast-feeding me as she held me with her sweetness.

Thank you, Grandmother Plum Tree, for your love and care and seeing me into manhood and the Medicine of Walking Crow, Transformational Sacred Drum Medicine.

I love you and will love you always,
your eternal son ~Walking Crow.

About the Author

Anthony J Rodriguez was born February 24, 1961 in San Fernando, California and began his life living in the nearby suburb of Pacoima.

As a young man battling drug addictions and alcoholism, he was arrested for driving drunk and very quickly found himself sober, beginning a new life. Getting married several times and eventually divorcing each, Anthony was given energy healing by a friend, and the experience changed his life. He moved in a direction he didn't even know was possible. It set him on a new path of transformation and change. Because of that healing session, he decided to become an energy healer and found a school that would teach him how.

As he began transforming his life, he found the Red Road and the indigenous teachings of the natives of Turtle Island (the Americas). Anthony eventually developed his own way of healing called Transformational Sacred Drum Medicine. Many teachers appeared, but most important to him was Rev. Emma Molina-Ynequez, who eventually named him Walking Crow.

Walking Crow has helped others from all over the world, offering healing sessions, mentoring, ceremony, teaching, working with the emotional body, making drums and rattles and being a hollow bone continuing to transform and help others to do the same.

"I have transformed from a seemingly hopeless state of mind and body. I was never hopeless, I was only helpless. I asked for help and I remain hopeful."

~ Walking Crow
Transformational Sacred Drum Medicine
Sedona, Arizona

Made in the USA
Columbia, SC
02 July 2024